Dear John,

Thx for your expol

Nick

25

Best Practices
in
Learning & Talent Development

Nick van Dam

All royalties from this book will be donated to the **e-Learning For Kids** (**www.e-learningforkids.org**) a global non-profit foundation that provides children (5–12) with high quality online learning for free.

This book is dedicated to children—
Our Talent for the Future . . . .

Lulu Publishers
www.lulu.com
Email: orders@lulu.com

Printed in USA

ISBN: 978-1-4303-1740-1

Contents

Multi-Cultural Perspectives in Learning

Leveraging the Business Impact of Learning

The Future of Learning and Talent Development

Acknowledgements

The best practices in this book have been written over a period of about two years. It takes lot of reading, observing, talking and reflection to develop a selection of best practices or trends. Ideally, I like to bounce around a lot of ideas and get feedback from a number of people in my network. This sharpens my thinking and helps me to identify weak spots, as well as additional perspectives.

My friend Eileen Rogers has been extremely valuable in fine tuning and validating my ideas for best practices. I have great memories of many conversations where we played around with a number of ideas and always built on each others insights and strengths. I want to thank Eileen for all of this and for creating and putting many best practice trends into action in the design of world-class leadership programs. Also, deep gratitude for editing the final version of the manuscript for this book.

I am thankful for the opportunity to collaborate with a number of Deloitte colleagues and true professionals on different subjects, who greatly contributed through their research and work in this area. Several are due special thanks. Robin Athey, Director of Deloitte Research, for her work on Performance Management. Robin has a true *research mind* and comes always up with new and intriguing questions. Mary Andrade, a pioneer and leader in designing classroom simulations. These learning interventions have proven to be extremely powerful and make a true difference in learning. Stan Smith, the Deloitte Director of New Generation Initiatives. Stan has contributed significant insights in his outstanding work on Generation Y. The impact of this new work-force on organizations in careers, learning and development cannot be underestimated.

Thanks to all my respected colleagues at Deloitte in Learning and Talent Management and our Human Capital Practice. All of you have been a source of inspiration, particularly, colleagues who are part of my

Deloitte Learning and Talent Development Management Team including: Melinda Adams, Diego Anchelerguez, Cissy Chiu, Tony Gleeson, Doina Patrubani, Annie Tobias, Robert Tweedy, and Kathy Scholz. Without their valuable insights, professionalism and drive, we would not have been able to implement these best practices within Deloitte.

Thanks to Jeff Schwartz, Bill Pelster and Joshua Haims for all of our collaborative, valuable experiences with clients.

Jim Wall, Global Managing Director Human Resources for Deloitte Touche Tohmatsu, has been a fantastic mentor, who has provided me with the opportunity to leverage my talent to the maximum within Deloitte. Hadewig Dokter for sharing your insights and experiences in talent branding and development.

Thanks also to Dre Kampfraath for making this book come to life with a number of illustrations done on his own time to support the e-Learning For Kids Foundation, and my friend Sushant Buttan for acquiring support from Aptara for the lay-out of this book.

I would like to thank the volunteer management team from the e-Learning For Kids Foundation: Tara Bryan, Amy Castillo, Vicki Cerda, David Dun, Michelle Hancock, Veronica Inoue, Brian Petersen, Dhannya Sekhar, and Julia Taylor. It has been such a pleasure to build the e-Learning For Kids Foundation with all of you. It's all to your credit what has been accomplished.

Finally, I want especially to thank my wife, Judith Grimbergen, for the design of the cover of the book, and for supporting my passion to work on this book in the limited time that is typically left in any week.

This book captures a collection of Best Practices in Learning & Talent Development that I have seen implemented in leading enterprises including Deloitte. I have published several of these best practices, sometimes in a condensed version, in my column 'Trends' in CLO Magazine, and believe that a collection of the best approaches to learning & talent development will contributed some insights in our complex and demanding world.

What a fantastic time for any professional to be involved in Talent Development. Most organizations are in a very early stage of adoption of new ways of designing and implementing new learning interventions, and the ability to be involved in the creation and implementation of new approaches to learning, growth, career development and business impact is extraordinary.

I hope that you will find some of the best practices introduced in this book useful in energizing your vision and your practice in empowering people performance.

You can find new and updated best practices on Learning & Talent Development on my website: www.nickvandam.com. I would appreciate it if you would share some of your own success stories and/or provide me with any feedback. Just send me an email: nvandam@ deloitte.com

Nick

February 2008   Hilversum, The Netherlands

Introduction

The Strategic Role of Learning & Talent Development

Over the coming 20 years, a wealth of experience and knowledge is expected to walk out of the door in many organizations. By 2011 an estimate of 75 million positions will become vacant due to retiring baby boomers in the European Union and the United States, of which an expected 40 percent represent people in (senior) management roles. At the same time, global competition, complexity and accelerated technology will drive the need for more *tacit* work – work with complex interactions that require a high level of judgment. Significantly, there will be less qualified candidates on the planet to replace these retiring baby boomers. Even China with its 1.3 billion+ population expects a drop in their workforce because of an aging workforce and their 'one child policy'. Global shortages of qualified employees are expected in many industries and professions. Already 79 percent of companies see a significant gap in the talent pipeline and 40 of the companies say this is an acute problem. As the market for talent heats up, organizations are looking at ways to attract people and develop their next generation of leaders.

What Does Talent Want?

Different research studies show that people expect interesting and challenging work with opportunities for growth and development. They would like to work in value-based enterprises which contribute to the welfare of overall society. They also want respect for their individual talent and an open communication with their management. Surveys among graduates show that, in addition to what has mentioned before, the new workforce wants to be part of an international organization and build their careers by extending their professional network. More and more people value a deep investment in their personal life in addition to enjoying a challenging work environment.

It also is becoming widely recognized that the most important way to engage employees is to provide them with opportunities to learn and develop new skills, providing ways to improve their capabilities and skills over their accomplishments of prior years (Towers Perrin, 2006). Highly engaged employees have a significant impact on the productivity and performance of an organization. Furthermore, engaged employees are more likely to stay with the organization where they are being challenged and given the skills to grow and develop in their chosen career path.

Shareholders will look more and more at the role of intangible assets when they value knowledge-based organizations. For example, at least 50 percent of market capitalization in America's public companies is due to skilled workforce and know-how (intangible assets). Globally this is up from 20 percent of the value of companies in 1980 to 70 percent today.

These economic, demographic and social trends support the expectation that Learning and Talent Development will play a more strategic role in many enterprises.

Strategic Role of Learning and Talent Development

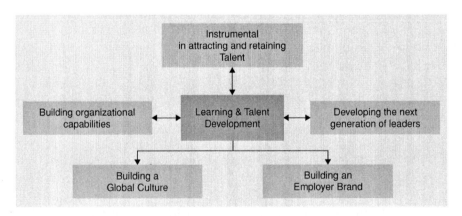

There are a number of forces that will require organizations to take a very different approach in developing their people.

First, due to a combination of pressures including the brief shelf life of knowledge, the pressure of new legislation to develop specific understanding and skills, the need to fill the gap in knowledge and expertise created by retiring baby boomers, introduction of new technologies, alternative business models, and globalization, to name a few, there is a need to master more competences and develop new skills. Secondly, the Internet has changed the way people acquire knowledge, learn and collaborate around the world. About 40 percent of learning hours were delivered through technology-based learning in the United States in 2007 (ASTD). Third, we moving more towards a 24/7 global society where people need to develop new competences and skills on the fly and there will be a big shift towards workplace learning. Fourth, Generation Internet, people born after 1980, are joining the workforce. They have very different expectations about work, and their learning preferences are very different as well.

Finally and importantly, advances in theory and practice in designing effective learning provide opportunities to develop high impact learning interventions that have a significant impact on individual performance and the business.

Developing 21st Century Leaders

If your actions inspire others to dream more, learn more, do more and become more, you are a leader.

John Quincy Adams

A Holistic Approach for Leadership Development

A challenge for those of us who are working in leadership development in our organizations is the narrow focus on acquisition of knowledge for leaders. We must expand the vision to address the complex requirements in an intensive effort to create a business case for a comprehensive, holistic approach in the growth of leadership talent.

There has not been a time in business history when so many senior leaders have voluntarily left their organizations. Leaders today must cope with an increasingly broad range of complex challenges including: a fast changing and uncertain business environment, pressures from internal and external stakeholders, emerging competition from new geographies, the rapid pace of technical innovation, and the importance of retaining talent, among others. This limits in some the desire to pursue a highly visible leadership role. Additionally, many leaders from the baby boom generation are getting ready for retirement – which will result in significant knowledge and experience gaps.

Because of these two trends, organizations are now experiencing a crisis of leadership talent, surfacing the questions: *How can we speed up the development of new leaders*? And even more difficult: *What makes a good leader in this complex century?*

There are no simple or easy answers. Enterprises are making serious investments in leadership development and succession planning, leadership gurus are developing leadership models, frameworks and assessments, and leadership development groups are creating innovative programs. Yet, controversy prevails, as some believe that leadership talent is inborn, not made, and that no amount of investment can create a leader.

It is my enduring belief that leadership is not an inherent talent but that leadership can be developed. The fact that leaders with different personalities and styles have succeeded throughout history, provides evidence that a specific crisis or context can leverage individual leadership strengths and capabilities, uncovering innate leadership talent. However, when the situation demanding a leader and specific leadership styles and approaches are analyzed, it becomes very apparent that throughout the leader's life there have been significant investments in developing individual leadership values, knowledge, attributes and talents.

Learning professionals often focus on leadership development in terms of the intellectual realm only. This limits the growth and development of leadership talent – leadership is seen and developed as an academic pursuit of the mind, versus development of the leader as a holistic instrument. Personally, I don't believe anyone ever followed a leader just because of their intellect and knowledge. I believe that people align themselves with a leader more as a function of connections formed in the emotional, social and/or spiritual realms.

Therefore, my goal is to pursue the creation and application of a more holistic leadership development framework in the design of leadership programs, which addresses four critical dimensions of leadership development for the 21st century:

- Intellectual Understanding
- Emotional and Social Competence
- Physical and Mental Health
- Spiritual Insight

A 21st Century Holistic Leadership Development Model

Intellectual Understanding

The intellectual development of a leader focuses on strategic thinking – the acquisition of new knowledge, and industry and business insights – typically delivered by subject matter experts in business and by faculty in business school executive education programs. The main objective is to bring leaders up to speed in areas where they lack knowledge for their existing role, or to prepare them for a larger role in the organization. Most importantly, the acquisition of this knowledge is increased when action learning on real-time strategic projects is embedded in the learning.

Emotional and Social Competence

Getting things done in enterprises and working through issues of transformational change requires leaders who have superior skills in establishing and maintaining relationships with others. In order to do so, leaders must have a solid understanding of how their actions and behaviors impact others. Secondly, they need to understand how they are perceived by others. The notion of emotional intelligence has emerged as a critical area for leadership development in many organizations as it is the foundation for high performance interpersonal skill development and an EQ focus is included in many leadership development programs and executive coaching.

Physical and Mental Health

Many leaders work long and demanding days, sometimes combined with intensive (international) travel and irregular times for exercise, relaxation and even meals. Research has reinforced that retaining a healthy body and mind demands taking regular time for physical exercise, relaxation and stress reduction, and carefully watching individual diet. Awareness and development in physical and mental health must be an important aspect of leadership programs, and can be incorporated through experiential learning initiatives.

Spiritual Insight

Spiritual development to a large extent centers on the personal values of leaders. *What is important for them in life? What do they want to achieve personally? How do they envision their legacy? How do they treat people? What's their vision on the world and the environment? How do they connect with people?* Personal values are developed over time through a combination of: the family they grew up in, their life experiences and important events, religious beliefs, relationships with friends, and business experience, among others. *Why is spiritual development of leaders important?* Personal values and beliefs impact judgment, decisions and behaviors, the organizational culture, and leaders lead by example. Therefore leader behaviors and actions are carefully watched and followed by others in the organization, creating the organizational climate and the overall (ethical) culture in the organization.

The complex demands of the 21st century require leaders who are skilled and aware in all four areas, and yet the challenge for those of us who are working in leadership development in our organizations is the currently limited focus on the acquisition of knowledge for leaders. We must expand the vision in an intensive effort to create a business case for a comprehensive, holistic approach in the growth of leadership talent.

Typically, bright leaders are very comfortable in the academic, knowledge-based intellectual realm which lends itself perfectly for speed of implementation. The spiritual and emotional realms require one to pause and reflect. In these arenas, leaders must slow down in order to speed up. This can be more challenging. There are no shortcuts in the emotional and social, spiritual, or physical and mental health realms. However, a true leader embraces all four areas as important to their individual development, and the rewards are considerable once one embraces them. The challenge is to generate support among business leaders for the exploration into these realms as a valid, productive aspect of leadership development.

Building Leaders Over Time

Taking full advantage of 21st century learning technologies, an extended learning continuum approach provides opportunities to embed learning in day-to-day realities and practices, while it maximizes the time of busy participants in the mastery of new knowledge, skills and behaviors.

It is common knowledge, supported by cutting-edge research, that leaders learn the most when they are on-the-job. Best practices in many enterprises indicate that the best approach to building leaders is to target and pursue learning that provides an opportunity to apply key leadership capabilities on teams, in projects and with clients.

A leadership learning strategy that is delivered in a 'blended' solution harnesses the application of best practices and employs multiple methodologies for learning, thus extending the learning continuum beyond the classroom event. This provides more potential for leaders to master new leadership behaviors, skills and attitudes where it counts – on-the-job.

The Leadership Development Model identifies the steps that are fundamental to good learning practice in creating a leadership development program.

Leadership Development Model

- **Link learning to the core values of the organization.**
  Corporate scandals combined with public opinion have put company core values and ethical behaviors at the center of every organization. Leaders must lead by example and develop a value-based enterprise. Therefore, core values are the integrating foundation for leadership development programs.

- **Ensure that the business strategy is driving the learning agenda.**
  Leaders drive the development and execution of the company's strategy. Leadership programs inform and engage leaders on the elements of the strategy and enable them to master the implementation challenges.

- **Conduct needs analysis and determine current capability levels.**
  Once the core values are embedded and the connection to execution of the business strategy is understood, it is critical to conduct a needs and capability analysis on comprehensive competencies. This enables the enterprise to determine where the actual real-time learning opportunities would produce the maximum results.

- **Select content and design a learning continuum.**
  Based on the assessment and analysis, one can create a leadership model that encompasses the capabilities required for success in the enterprise. This provides a framework for the leadership learning content.

- **Extend the learning beyond the classroom to the job.**
  Provide a learning continuum that is of high quality through online learning resources and coaching that extends the learning into the workplace and makes learning available just-in-time.

In our highly demanding world, there seems to be little time or support for leaders to reflect on learning experiences and to integrate new knowledge into their enterprises. This decreases the potential value of leadership development programs to the extent that business leaders question the business return-on-investment of funds allocated to leadership development.

Meeting this challenge, a number of organizations and leading business schools are implementing a new learning model for leadership development. This is a learning continuum that extends the leadership learning benefits and value over time, supporting deeper integration of the skills and knowledge into individual performance, business application and bottom-line results.

Taking full advantage of 21st century learning technologies, this approach provides opportunities to embed learning in day-to-day realities and practices, while it maximizes the time of busy participants in the mastery of new knowledge, skills and behaviors.

When designing an *extended leadership development program* one can consider the following elements:

Pre-Program Learning

- **Learning Community of Practice**
  All people who have signed up for the program join a learning community that remains in place for some time before and post-program. This network provides opportunities for individuals to share knowledge and build on their joint learning experiences.

- **Virtual Classroom Modules**
  Virtual classroom sessions are used to engage participants with the faculty in discussions of important topics, investigation of various insights and perceptions, and in reviewing the relevance of assigned online learning readings, courses, and assessments.

- **Online Courses and Self Study**
  Leaders have differing educational backgrounds and levels of prior knowledge. The classroom experience is most valuable for peer exchange and the application of concepts, behaviors, and knowledge to real-time leadership and business challenges. Online learning modules, webinars, and other self-study guides ensure that individual participants have attained a shared level of understanding and knowledge about key topics prior to joining the group in the classroom.

- **Online Assessments**
  A thorough understanding of existing leadership skills and competencies is important in the identification of individual capabilities and knowledge gaps which drive learning. Online assessment tools provide opportunities for personal insights and for receiving

feedback from a number of resources. In addition, the completion and processing of online surveys and assessments does not impact time dedicated to the classroom.

Post-Program Learning

- **Managing Individual Goals**
  Programs only make business sense if individuals can apply acquired knowledge and skills in the workplace, having a measurable impact on business performance. Therefore, it is highly recommended that individuals set a number of specific goals after the program. Online goal setting and performance can enable the progress and achievement of these goals to be shared among the program cohort, with other leaders and supervisors, and feedback on goal progress can be posted and supported online.

- **Action Learning**
  Real-time strategic projects, either on an individual or team basis, allow the leaders to dedicate time and resources to critical issues of importance to the business. This practice integrates learning into actual results that benefit the future success of the enterprise.

- **Expand the Knowledge Base**
  When participants begin to apply knowledge gained from the learning program to their work, they identify specific subject areas where deeper and broader investigation is of great benefit. Specific new learning content is made available and is targeted to individuals based on their identified needs.

- **Executive Coaching**
  Limited time is available for leaders to coach other leaders. External executive coaches fill this gap and provide the individual with a structured approach for achieving their personal goals. The executive coach can also be a strong subject matter expert who helps the individual to lead in new area.

- **Learning Community of Practice**
  As program alumni, it is very valuable to reconnect with the program cohort through a sharing of post-program experiences, through action learning projects, and by reaching out for input related to specific issues, leveraging this learning network for new expertise.

Building leaders requires a complete analysis of the development needs of leaders and aligning these with the strategy of the enterprise. The design of an extended learning program can provide a rich learning experience which supports application of knowledge and addresses the enterprise challenges of limited time, cost reduction and extension of learning over multiple geographies. The next Best Practice section investigates how this is accomplished in a fully blended leadership development model.

Blended Leadership Development Programs

Well-designed blended leadership programs have proven to be an extremely powerful learning experience that pushes the learning boundaries well beyond the classroom, incorporating leadership learning and development into business realities and results.

Today's organizations recognize that the turbulence of global markets, competition, geopolitics, and the shortage of talent require focused, skilled leadership to survive and succeed. Leadership development is increasingly regarded as the platform needed to grow and improve the business. No longer an exclusive privilege of senior executives, leadership development is being employed to embed the capabilities required to achieve strategic goals, organize innovative projects, change culture and cascade competencies throughout the organization. Major companies are pursuing key themes in the development of their leaders. To maximize the link between leadership capabilities and strategy execution, **leader-led** development is being used to engage senior executives in the training and coaching of the next generation of leadership. The use of **team business projects** during leadership programs focuses participants on strategy execution while solving real-time problems and challenges. Also, a **learning continuum** for leadership development is being pursued by most organizations as they have found they need to embed behavioral change and new strengths and perspectives requires more than a one-week event. In addition, recognizing that the development of leaders demands the best talent in leader learning and development, the importance of selecting experienced **external partners** is seen as a critical cornerstone.

To accomplish this intensive, ongoing leadership development over a period of time with busy, geographically dispersed executives and leaders is a daunting task. However, organizations that have used e-Learning in a blended model for leadership in a learning continuum have found that this approach supports:

- Leveraging the time executives have available to engage in learning.
- Virtual teamwork on business and individual projects.
- Online coaching and mentoring by senior executives.
- Online collaboration promoting post-program virtual work.
- Enhancing the quality of the learning experience.
- Reducing costs.

Design and development of blended leadership programs is definitely a new competency for program designers and business schools. The graphic below shows an example of the activity flow of a blended leadership program. A blended model of learning uses an engaging combination of self-paced e-Learning, face-to-face and experiential learning, live e-Learning classes, assessments, readings, coaching, project teamwork and online collaboration and sharing of best practices.

Participant engagement and progress is closely monitored by a learning program manager who facilitates the learning process, provides constant feedback and guidance, and reports on progress made to the participant's executive counselor.

Blended Leadership Development Continuum

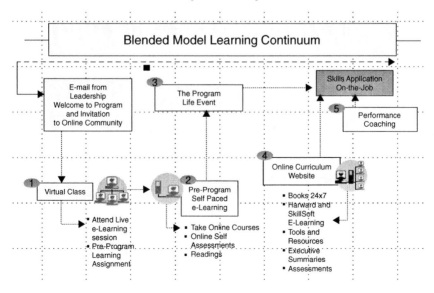

The *blended* leadership learning model is delivered over time in five main steps.

- **Launch leadership learning with a virtual class:** A high touch involvement with leaders demonstrating a true understanding of their world and challenges is vital to success of the leader's commitment to the process. Launching the learning continuum with a virtual class establishes the community of learning and ensures understanding of the value of the time commitment to the learning.

- **Push out self-paced online learning:** A rich combination of online leadership assessment and individual leadership style reports, e-Learning courses, with readings and Internet resources are provided with an opportunity to interact with the learning coaches.

- **Conduct the classroom program:** This highly valuable time is focused on peer knowledge exchange, problem-solving and action planning along with practice application of new skills and performance coaching, building the culture and professional networks.

- **Support on-the-job learning with targeted online learning:** Based on specific development and learning needs, targeted online, self-paced learning is pushed out to participants to incorporate learning on-the-job. Also, online learning guides provide self-service access to multiple resources by leadership topic for just-in-time learning.

- **Coaching and Performance Support:** Participants can set specific performance goals at the end of a program based on developed skills and acquired insights during the learning program. Performance coaches check in with program alumni on progress made, obstacles encountered and provide support to apply new skills in their work.

Furthermore, a Leadership Learning Map available online offers just-in-time learning when leaders return to their jobs. A click on a button on the map opens doors of targeted learning to selected e-Learning leadership courses, and access to leading business publications, executive summaries of business best-selling books, and business articles and assessments. Topics for leaders might include: Influence and Persuasion, Emotional Intelligence, and Building your Leadership Brand.

Example of a Leadership Learning Map

Leadership Excellence Learning Map

Topic	Foundation	Mastery
Core Leadership	Leadership Roles and Capabilities	
	Leading With Vision	Masterful Communication
	Global Citizenship	Leading Innovation and Change
	Building Relationships	Mentoring Growth and Development
Leadership Skills	Persuasion and Influence	Trust and Authenticity
	Negotiation and Consensus	Leading with Emotional Intelligence
Business Development	Leading The Professional Service Firm	
	Client-Centric Sales	Leading Knowledge Wo
Leadership Brand	Your Leadership Brand	

One of the advantages of a blended leadership program is that it is not just an "event"; rather, it can be a one- or two-year leadership development continuum by leadership level.

Well-designed blended leadership programs have proven to be an extremely powerful learning experience that pushes the learning boundaries well beyond the classroom, incorporating leadership learning and development into business realities and results.

Developing The Leader's Core Strengths

Research in neuroscience tells us that a person's talent does not change significantly over time, and that leaders will improve the most in their areas of greatest talent. This implies a very different approach to leadership development, performance management and career planning.

A child with great talent in soccer will most likely be encouraged to play soccer rather than becoming a champion swimmer. A great skier will probably not become a star basketball player. What makes common sense in the world of sports – that each person should 'play to their strengths' – is counterintuitive to business practices in performance management, appraisal, development and promotion. Rather than a focus on how we can offer opportunities and challenges in business that *'play to individual strengths'*, organizational performance systems tend to focus on developing people in areas where they are weak, and many times firms promote them when they are strong performers into new jobs that don't support the use of their inherent strengths.

In widely used performance appraisal processes, managers discuss people's performance and rate them in different competency areas against an existing framework. A primary objective is to identify areas for improvement. Inevitably, a development plan is created focusing the individual on developing capabilities where they are deficient because the organization has put future measures, evaluations and incentives behind this. In addition, people who have performed very well in a current role are most likely to be rewarded and moved into a new position for which they might not have the requisite talent, knowledge and skills. Ironically, a large number of outstanding performers might end up as amateurs in the enterprise, and even fail in important roles in their career, because advancement places them in positions that reflect their non-strengths, and those who continue doing what they are very good at and known for, often find their careers stalled.

One of the key questions we may ask is: *What would be best way to develop people with the highest possible impact on individual growth and development and with the best outcomes for the organization?*

Neuroscience research has shown that from birth to 3 years of age, the brain grows exponentially in billions of synaptic connections. Then between the ages of 3 and 15, the brain organizes itself by strengthening the synaptic connections that are used frequently, while those that are used infrequently wither away. In other words, roads with most traffic get widened and others are closed. (Harry T. Chugani, Wayne State University School of Medicine) Strong evidence exists that beyond a person's mid-teens, this unique network of synaptic connections does not alter greatly. Basically, people's inherent characteristics or talents are solidified, and the more that these are engaged, and the more they are preferred, the stronger they become.

When this is applied to workers in the business world, you will find that those people who you hire as strong communicators will stay strong communicators. People with strong creative skills will continue to be creative. A pioneer in identifying this concept of knowledge, skill and talents built through practice into strengths and applying this understanding to business is The Gallup organization. Gallup has completed more than 40 years of study in this area, and has labeled recurring patterns of thoughts, feeling or behavior as *talents*. These inherent talents, acquired knowledge and related skills, when developed and utilized, become *strengths*. Gallup has defined a strength as: *'the greatness that consistently delivers a positive outcome through near-perfect performance, every time'*. Based on the work of Donald Clifton, Gallup has also realized that when explicit investments are made in identifying worker strengths and ensuring that their job supports, challenges and grows these strengths, they will become star performers.

Nevertheless, people can definitely change and can develop new skills and knowledge . However, a key question arises: *Which development opportunity provides the biggest impact, investments in areas of deficiency or in strengths?*

Neuroscience research finds that we should identify people's talent and provide people with development experiences that build on strengths to create consistently excellence performances. Naturally, people will always try to spend time in their talented areas. This is where their energy and passion flows and what they most enjoy doing. *But is this practical and possible in the world of organizational roles and responsibilities?*

In a talent-driven organization, there is a deliberate focus on a leader's strengths, yielding interesting possibilities and results. First, it is especially beneficial to identify specific capabilities and ensure that the role and the responsibilities of the position play the leader's passion, strengths and interests. Also, it is possible to apply areas of strength that seem unrelated in creative ways to the job. However, this can only occur if the strengths are known and an explicit dialogue and focus helps the leader to see how the strength can be utilized successfully. Finally, training and learning can be accessed to both build areas of inherent strength, but also to build strength intentionally in areas that must be performed, and cannot be delegated to someone else, enough so that the deficiency does not impact overall performance. Job sculpting also plays a role and forward-looking organizations ensure that their top talent are known for what they do best, and receive assignments that enable them to play to these strengths.

Several steps are required to move towards a more *'talent-driven'* career growth and development strategy:

- **People need to identify their areas of greatest strength.**
  When people know and have a language to describe their strengths and the application of this strength to a role or a task, the organization can be very focused on ensuring that their work offers opportunities to grow in the areas where they can be star performers. This can be done by asking others about their strengths and/or by using a diagnostic tool to identify these strengths. (For instance Gallup's StrengthsFinder® diagnostic).

- **Assess if people leverage their strengths in their role.**
  In a research survey, only 20 percent of people answered that they 'strongly agree' on the statement: *"At work, I have the opportunity to do what I do best every day"*. (Gallup). This shows that most people are not in roles where they can build on their strengths. Therefore, leaders should explore which strengths can be used in their roles, or if they should pursue a different role within their organization.

- **Help people to focus on their strengths.**
  The organization must help leaders to understand the impact of a strength-based approach to their performance. For example, leaders should spend about 80 percent of their time on building their talents by acquiring relevant skills, knowledge and experience. Additionally, they should focus on learning and development in areas where the weakness stems from a lack of skills or knowledge, building capabilities only to the extent required so that it is not a barrier to performance, and quickly returning to capitalizing on strengths.

Finally, if enterprises want to build a world-class organization and retain their best talent, they must promote high performing leaders into roles where they can continue to leverage their strengths. Traditional career and promotion paths must be replaced by development opportunities and career moves which support each individual's unique strengths and their inherent talents.

Accelerated Development

There is a fundamental shift taking place in the way we work. The corporate work force has, in a few short generations, completely transformed itself. These changes have been triggered by work force shortages, the interaction of different generations in the workplace, globalization and technological innovations. Accelerated development can develop individual potential faster, provide the knowledge and experience that people need and build a strong leadership pipeline.

We need skilled workers and we need to accelerate the development of our new and existing people to ensure that they can take on new roles faster and capture the rich body of knowledge and expertise from the retiring baby boomers in our enterprises. But how can we accomplish this? And what are the key talent management instruments that need to be implemented in enterprises?

- Identification of key talent linked to succession planning and strategy execution

- Performance motivation and management

- Development through mobility, learning and coaching

People can be identified for new and/or expended roles through well executed performance management and succession management processes. Most companies skilled in this know who their high performers are – typically 5–15% of the workforce. Furthermore, the top talent among the high performers must be identified and linked to the succession plan. Only if the current leadership is engaged in the identification and preparation of these future leaders can this truly succeed. Those in the leadership pipeline can be identified in two tiers: those who could function immediately and are essentially *ready now* and those who, with more development and experience, could be *ready later*.

The highly talented people who are *ready later* are then targeted intentionally for new assignments that focus on key developmental tasks. It is becoming apparent through decades of research and our own career experiences that the most important way to develop people is rotation into different roles, and in our global age, across boundaries. Working with a new team, a different division/department, location or country in a new stretch assignment takes people out of their *comfort zone* and moves them into a *learning zone*.

Highly talented performers are then prepared for a future stretch assignment by assessing key competencies that they need to master the new role. Based on the competency gap, an individual development plan is prepared. This plan could be a combination of a number of different activities including:

- Working with an (executive) coach who will provide business coaching

- On-the-job mentoring from a trusted and more senior leader

- Personal leadership assessments which provide better insight in development needs of the leader. Social and emotional intelligence is a great predictor of future performance of the leader.

- Participation in specific learning and leadership programs which support developmental goals

Accelerated development of people is well supported if people have access to knowledge and learning which they need to do their job at the time they need it. Online learning plays an important role as it will provide the just-in-time and compressed learning for rapid skill development. For instance – a powerful resource for accelerated development is to provide access to leadership portals that provide a rich portfolio of leadership focused webinars, articles, blogs, podcasts, among others. Furthermore – virtual coaching has become a best practice as a scalable solution for the development and support of leaders.

However, much is required of the individuals beyond what the organizational processes, systems and capabilities can offer . . . it requires *career entrepreneurship* – those willing to take the risks and opportunities in a career progression that does not follow the traditional stepping stones. And this is the greatest challenge to organizations.

Can large-scale enterprises provide the assignments that do not follow lock step career advancement and become more entrepreneurial in considering what constitutes a successful career path, or must these talented individuals leave and join smaller organizations to progress?

In summary – a number of talent management capabilities must be in place to support the accelerated development of the workforce including: understanding the current capabilities of the workforce and roles needed in the future organization, performance and succession management processes and systems, people and leadership development capabilities, coaching, and online learning solutions. In addition, the organization must consider the current path to the top and assess in what ways it is supportive of accelerated development and what barriers it either intentionally or unintentionally poses to the advancement of the most talented. Accelerated development can develop individual potential faster, provide the knowledge and experience that people need and build a strong leadership pipeline, only if our organizations can create a vibrant, dynamic view of entrepreneurial, individualized and empowering career paths.

Developing Scalable Business Coaching

Most are familiar with Yoda, the stern and benevolent coach of the Jedi knights in Star Wars. Because of his age and experience, Yoda is selected to train the Jedi knights who will vanquish the dark force. In a key scene, Luke Skywalker, the young Jedi, tells Yoda he will try and Yoda responds, 'Do or do not, there is no try.' This is the key task of the coach, to enable others to realize they have the potential to succeed in the difficult tasks and transitions of life, and empower them to act on the basis of strengths.

Although there are many styles of coaching today – sports, life, dating, business, and executive, among others – to identify one's passion in work and develop a career, the business coach relationship is critical. The task of the business coach is similar to Yoda's, to enable others to discover their capabilities, define their aspirations, and develop personal belief to pursue personal career goals with confidence.

Careers have become incredibly complex in the 21st century global economy. Today a career is comprised of personal ownership – no longer a lock-step progression to the top – and skilled navigation through uncharted opportunity. As described by Cathy Benko, Chief Talent Officer for Deloitte in her publication, Mass Career Customization, the career ladder has morphed into the career lattice, where the experience is: *'No longer a straight climb up the corporate ladder, careers are more commonly an undulating journey of climbs and lateral moves.'* (www.masscareercustomization.com) In addition, the global economy poses enormous potential for personal opportunity – driving a global war for talent.

This intersection between the desire for personal career flexibility and the global potential for growth and development, demands that each enterprise engage and retain key talent through flexible career paths and skilled business coaching. Having the opportunity to develop a career with a business coach can be the one connection to the organization that strengthens both the contribution to work and employee engagement. However, reaching each individual with a business coach relationship in the global enterprise can be difficult – complicated by language, culture, time zones, and distance, among others.

Scalable Business Coaching offers a powerful solution, once again harnessing the capabilities of the Internet with personal one-on-one and peer coaching sessions. The Business Coaching Portal can include opportunities for self-development, access to personal career and/or leadership coaching, links to internal job opportunities for internal mobility, virtual workshops for peer coaching, coach training and internal capabilities. Within each of these might be:

- **Self-Development:** Self-Assessments, Leadership 360°, Learning and Development Programs, Online Career Goals development and a creation of a Career Plan.

- **Business Coach:** One-on-one coaching to encourage ownership and personal navigation of career paths, to enable internal mobility, to develop leadership capability of top talent, and to support direction to external opportunity if desired. These coaches can be engaged in a global context to meet language, culture and time zone variations.

- **Virtual Career Development Workshops:** Sessions facilitated by a coach to discuss common career planning and development, sharing experiences and best practices among colleagues.

- **Coach Training:** Workshops and training to extend coaching in all relationships to foster teamwork, manage and inspire high performance, work effectively with others internal and external to the organization.

- **Links to Related Internal Capabilities:** Competency frameworks and processes, internal job postings, articles related to coaching, learning portal, requirements for internal and international transfers, career networks, and other

There is always a discussion on the differences among a coach, mentor and counselor, and these are highly different, yet overlapping, roles. According the International Coach Federation, http://www.coachfederation.org/ICF/, a business coach establishes an on-going partnership with the client through listening, observation and customization of their approach, enabling the client to identify their own career solutions and strategies, based on the belief that each individual has the skills, resources and talent to achieve their goals. Whereas, mentorship is a voluntary relationship between a more experienced mentor with a less experienced protégé, and a counselor is one who balances performance support on a specific career role or assignment with performance evaluation.

In our complex global economy where new opportunities surface daily, the global worker demands flexibility, scalability, and job sculpting to ensure that they are developing and applying their strengths and talents every day and that their career matches their life goals and aspirations. All of the roles, coach, mentor and counselor are needed, however, the business coach is integral to enabling these coveted workers to chart their own course effectively in the midst of complicated choices by leading them through a process of self-discovery and fostering belief that they can navigate their careers with success.

The challenge of course is ... *Can global organizations flex and scale their employment processes, procedures and opportunities in a new business model that matches the demands of today's talent?*

The Impact of Learning in Performance Management

Those having torches, will pass them on to others.

Plato

Engaging Top Talent By Delivering What They Care About Most

As the competition for critical talent heats up, organizations must rethink the ways they manage talent. Firms must concentrate on the things that employees care about most:

- *Developing them in ways that stretch their capabilities.*
- *Deploying employees onto projects and jobs that engage their heads and hearts.*
- *Connecting individuals to the people who will help them to succeed.*

Globalization is a force for both collaboration and competition. It is also proving to set the stage for a contest for resources – both natural and human. In an age in which growth is largely a product of creative and technical advancements, companies must engage people as never before to innovate and grow. Only those companies that win the hearts and minds of their top talent will deliver value over both the short- and long-term.

The contest for human capital is evident everywhere, although the nature and significance of trends vary from country to country. Throughout the western world, the retirement of the Baby Boom generation will create large vacancies across industries. In Europe, that trend will be particularly potent due to low birth and immigration rates. In China, the single child policy has led to a deficit of skilled workers, especially in urban areas. These massive shifts in workplace population will be exacerbated by educational trends. In the United States and Japan, for example, the percentage of students graduating with science and engineering degrees hovers in the single digits, far below the percentage figures for India and China. Such trends suggest a talent market unlike any that we have seen.

The game is changing in other ways as well. Jobs are no longer static. Companies must continually train and develop employees if they are to keep pace with speed and complexity. They must create mobility to deploy people where they are needed most, while acknowledging that people perform best in work that taps their skills and passions. And they must connect people across businesses, divisions, and regions in ways that promote high quality decisions and fast execution. Responding to today's workplace means that firms must offer more than just a good paycheck. Record-high numbers of dissatisfied workers already cost organizations millions of dollars in lost productivity.

In the face of such challenges, traditional approaches to managing talent fall short. *Why is that so – and what must firms do? What do shifts in the way that we manage talent mean for Performance Management?*

In the 1990s, companies responded to shifting labor markets by launching a *'War for Talent'*. Today, bidding wars lead firms to spend 50 times more on recruiting than training. This sets firms up for an inevitable churn. Even the best recruitment tactics will not suffice in the struggle ahead. Rich compensation packages and *'hot skills'* bonuses are easily matched by competitors. Instead, a more thoughtful response is required – one that lures critical talent, but more importantly engages them in ways that promote the flexibility and productivity that firms need to innovate and grow.

As the competition for critical talent heats up, organizations must rethink the ways they manage talent. The traditional talent acquisition and management model is depicted below.

The Traditional Talent Management Process

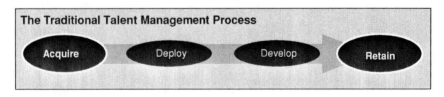

When talent becomes scarce, organizations focus their energy on *acquiring* and *retaining* talent. This focus on the end points is problematic because it diverts attention away from what matters most to people. That is – their development in ways that foster personal and professional growth, their deployment onto jobs that tap their skills and passions, and their connection to one another. When firms build strategies on what matters most to their employees, the best talent is engaged and decides to stay. In addition, the organization becomes simultaneously a more desirable employer for new talent. As a result, they find that metrics and outcomes such as acquisition and retention largely take care of themselves.

To begin, enterprises must identify the segments of the workforce that drive their current and future growth. These are not just the stars, or '*A players*', who are often the first to leave when other opportunities surface. Instead, they are the often overlooked people who create the value that leads to growth – educators, researchers, customer service professionals – whoever does the work that the market rewards for innovation and differentiation.

Then, rather than focus on acquisition and retention, the end points of the talent management process, firms must concentrate on the things that employees care about most:

- Developing them in ways that stretch their capabilities.
- Deploying employees onto projects and jobs that engage their heads and hearts.
- Connecting individuals to the people who will help them to succeed.

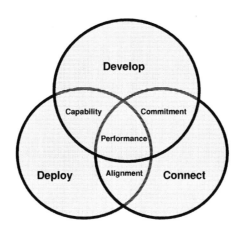

The Develop-Deploy-Connect Model

The Develop-Deploy-Connect model should be at the core of an organization's talent strategy. By focusing on these three elements, the linkages between the three realms generate employee capability, commitment and alignment, which in turn improves business performance. The potential for using this model with a new perspective on performance management will be discussed in the next best practice section.

The Develop-Deploy-Connect Process in Transforming Performance Management

Focusing on critical talent is relatively new territory for most companies, and thus, offers a new way to compete. Compared to investments in customer, technical, and financial strategies (which may become commoditized over time), a well-designed talent strategy can truly differentiate an organization.

Much has been published about performance management and there are different uses of the term, but the main characteristics of performance management include (Slottje 2003):

- An appraisal system (including goal setting).
- A reward system (including compensation).
- Assessment and feedback procedures (e.g., 360° degree assessments).
- Communication processes between employee and employer.

Broadly speaking, there are two issues with current approaches to learning and development in relation to performance management.

- To begin, significant energy is often spent on technology systems, and not enough is invested in human needs.
- Second, in our quest for metrics, great emphasis is placed on what can be easily measured (such as hours of training) and not enough on the skills and behavior that will enable organizations to master the trends ahead.

For example, globalization requires that individuals work effectively with colleagues halfway around the world. *Does the nature and quality of their interaction help them to build sustainable value? Is that recognized and rewarded?* The retirement of baby boomers means that the younger generation must learn how to apply the deep knowledge and experiences of veterans in new ways. *In what ways are older and younger generations proactively engaging with one another to ensure smooth succession? How do you assess progress?* An emerging skill gap means that people must learn faster, better, and more continuously than ever before. This must especially be the case for the people who will forge future growth. *If most of our learning is informal in nature, how well are they doing? How do you know?* Finally, leaders must enable people to create the conditions that work best for them given the shifting nature of work. *Are they succeeding? Are leaders throughout the organization (from the boardroom to the front lines) effectively coaching and developing those around them (direct reports and peers) in ways that promote organizational growth?*

One major risk of working in a 24/7 world is that we become more connected to each other technologically, but less connected to those who will make a difference. Indeed, the best approaches to performance management involve a careful balance of high-tech and high-touch. This balance recognizes that the most important aspect of performance management is often the performance dialogue that occurs. The system is only effective to the degree that it supports this conversation. Indeed, one large transport and logistics company has achieved stellar results by requiring performance conversations between managers and direct reports on a monthly basis. Workers are asked to spend at least one hour reflecting before each conversation. The result has led to a peak in profitability never before experienced in the 120 year old company.

Utilizing the Develop-Deploy-Connect Model to Engage Talent in Ways that Lead to Performance

Develop. Whether you're a CEO or machine specialist, work is getting faster and more complex. People's ability to do their jobs often depends on others halfway around the world. Jobs today require cognitive and analytical capability, personal skills, political savvy, influence and persuasion, delegation, adaptability, and cultural know-how. Such capabilities tend to be developed through experience, outside the physical or virtual classroom. We learn on-the-job, in the context of our work. We learn when we take risks. And we learn from our interactions with one another.

Given the nature of learning, why do we invest so much time, money and energy in training? It's often because training hours can be measured. On-the-job learning is harder to capture. Given the nature of emerging trends, though, leading firms recognize that learning is most effective when it is knitted into the fabric of people's projects, roles, and jobs. It is self-led, but also strategic and intentional. They build development plans around people's *experiences* – not just their skills or competencies. Individuals are coached to become more self-aware about their career interests and relationships. And rewards are given to those who promote knowledge sharing – whether it occurs in the corridor, at the water cooler, through mentoring programs, in communities of practice, or on the golf course.

Deploy. People learn the most in jobs that stretch them, and they perform the best when they actively define the roles that tap their deepest passions and skills. By and large, people are capable of doing many things. Indeed, some of the most successful people were never educated or trained for the roles they mastered. Mitch Kapor was a disk jockey and transcendental meditation teacher before he found the Lotus Development software company. David Ogilvy was a chef in Paris, a farmer in Pennsylvania, and a member of the British Intelligence agency before he made a fortune in advertising. Yet we have a tendency to pigeonhole people based on the confines of their resume. Finding one's career niche involves experimentation.

Leading organizations go to great lengths to help their talent find the roles and projects that engage their heads, hearts, and hands. Yet they don't allow such exploration to happen in an ad-hoc matter. Instead, they are very intentional about their approaches, finding ways to align individuals' interests with organizational goals. Engaging people in this way requires a clear strategy, good technology, and lots of dialogue. They build systems and processes to ensure that personal development plans align with strategic direction. But successful enterprise leaders don't wait for performance management systems to tell them when people are not aligned. They manage their talent on a real-time basis, employing dialogue and coaching to ensure that individuals head in directions that tap the best they have to offer.

Connect. As jobs become more complex, *who* you know is increasingly becoming more important than *what* you know. Career research suggests that our networks may be the most important determinant of professional success. People with rich and diverse networks develop social capital. This social capital helps them to land jobs and roles where they thrive. It also helps them to win the trust and support that they need to get results. To increase performance today, organizations must help key individuals to connect with the people and knowledge that they need to perform. They must also coach people to skillfully engage with others.

Research suggests that a tremendous amount of performance is lost due to miscommunication and toxic interactions. One study conducted by Rob Cross (University of Virginia) and Wayne Baker (University of Michigan) found that the *energizers* in an organization (i.e. those who energize the people around them) were four times more likely to be high performers than those who simply bring knowledge and skills to the table. Another study, conducted by Tiziana Casciaro (Harvard University) and Miguel Sousa Lobo (Duke University) found that the *lovable fools* in an organization tend to be higher performers than the *competent jerks*. People are drawn to people that they like and increasingly shun those who steal their energy. Tools such as social network analysis are proving immensely helpful in helping leaders to understand where the energy resides in their organizations – and where it is being sapped. Such feedback should become a core piece of performance management.

In the coming years, most companies will have no choice but to seriously rethink their talent and performance strategies. But shifting demographics should not be the only reason. Improving the performance of critical talent directly improves organizational performance. Furthermore, focusing on critical talent is relatively new territory for most companies, and thus offers a new way to compete. Compared to investments in customer, technical, and financial strategies (which may become commoditized over time), a well-designed talent strategy can truly differentiate an organization.

Globalization, the retirement of baby boomers, and a growing skill gap, create unprecedented pressure to attract and engage critical talent – those people who create the most value for organizations. Current approaches to performance management fall short in light of such trends.

What can enterprise leaders do? To begin, they must first examine their approaches to talent management, which often focus on the acquisition and retention of high-performers. Such tactics tend not to tap into what people need and expect from employers. Rather than focus on acquisition and retention – the end points of the talent management process – leaders must build strategies around the things that matter most to critical talent: their development in ways that foster personal and professional growth, their deployment onto jobs and projects that tap their skills and passions, and their connection to one another. Performance management must support this strategic approach.

Learning By Design

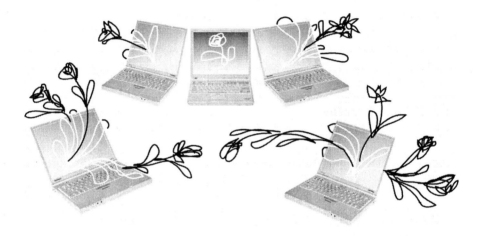

There is no such thing as information overload, just bad design.
Edward Tufte

The 21st Century Learning Capability Framework

Partnership with the business leaders relies upon a mutual understanding of the issues and the solutions – a shared language reflecting the strategic value of learning. The Learning Capability Framework illustrates and describes the multiple solutions available for both formal and self-directed learning, thus enabling this common language and clarifying the shared vision of a robust learning continuum.

The Chief Learning Officer (CLO) is the chief architect of the learning organization and must design learning interventions and solutions that support both *individual* learning, as well as *organizational* learning. Typically, business leaders have the belief that the learning function can only provide traditional learning solutions. However, the 21st century offers many effective learning approaches that go far beyond traditional learning solutions. Therefore, it is a primary task of the CLO to articulate a compelling vision of the role learning can play in strategic success and marketplace results, and the critical contribution learning can offer at the organizational level by employing new and creative learning solutions.

Reflecting on learning theory and practice, I have developed a simple framework that has proven useful in demonstrating to business leaders the extensive portfolio of potential learning solutions. This framework can become a powerful instrument for people in learning and talent management roles to share and illustrate the potential of the extended learning experience.

Learning Capability Framework

The **Learning Capability Framework** examines two dimensions of learning. The first dimension includes *Formal Learning Programs* which are created to support specific learning objectives and typically include instructional design approaches.

Examples of *Formal Learning Programs* include:

- **Classroom Programs and Workshops**
  Lecture-led, facilitated and simulation-based classroom programs.

- **Online and Mobile Learning**
  Self-paced e-Learning, virtual classroom, learning games, learning on PDA's and mobile phones, podcasts and videocasts.

- **Competency Assessments and Feedback**
  Various leadership and management surveys and assessment tools, for example: 360° Feedback, Emotional Intelligence, StrengthsFinder®, Myers-Briggs Type Indicator (MBTI®), and FIRO-B®, among others.

- **Learning Referenceware**
  Self-study guides and (online) study books.

- **On-The-Job Training**
  Specific training interventions designed to support learning at the workplace.

- **Executive Coaching**
  Formal, designed feedback and development processes for executives using a professional coach.

The second dimension of the **Learning Capability Framework** is *Self-Directed Learning* which does not require specific instructional learning design and supports informal learning.
   Examples of *Self-Directed Learning* solutions include:

- **Mentoring and Feedback**
  On-the-job development feedback from colleagues, and informal mentors.

- **Information Repositories**
  Access to various knowledge portals, databases and websites.

- **Communities of Practice**
  Self-organizing and self-directed groups of people informally bound together by a common vision and passion for a joint enterprise.

- **Expert Networks**
  Access to experts who share expertise and provide support for knowledge workers using a variety of collaboration and communication tools.

- **Performance Support Systems**
  Examples include: process embedded learning, job aids, check lists, online wizards, glossaries, and online applications and tools.

- **Search and Help**
  Using internal search engines and online help functions.

Ideally, both of the above dimensions of the framework are integrated with *Learning On-the-Job,* which many identify as the most valuable and important source of learning. In this area, **Communities of Practice** (often abbreviated as CoP) are perhaps the self-directed learning solution most directly linked to immediate, relevant and applied learning that enhances on-the-job performance. CoPs have been gaining much interest recently, primarily due the potential offered by worldwide web of linked computers to build an interactive, vibrant community dedicated to learning.

The concept of a CoP refers to the process of social learning that occurs when people who have a common interest in some subject or problem collaborate over an extended period to share ideas, find solutions, and build innovations. (Wikipidia) The term was first used in 1991 by Jean Lave and Etienne Wenger who used it in relation to *situated learning* as part of an attempt to "rethink learning" at the Institute for Research on Learning. Lave and Wenger find that everyone is intuitively and implicitly involved in multiple communities where they both contribute to, and engage in, learning from each other. Membership in these communities is voluntary and the value is defined by the activities and contributions of the members.

More recently, Communities of Practice have become associated with knowledge management, as people have begun to see them as ways of developing social capital, nurturing new knowledge, stimulating innovation, or sharing existing tacit knowledge within an organization. CoPs are now an accepted part of organizational development (Wiki red) and Lesser and Storck find that CoPs enable organizations to handle unstructured problems and to share knowledge outside of the traditional structural boundaries. In addition, it is found that the CoP is a means of developing and maintaining long-term organizational memory.

Until recently, the term *blended learning* was defined by learning professionals as the blend of classroom events with e-Learning. The truly valuable blend is a combination of <u>all</u> the learning solutions described in the **Learning Capability Framework**. In the place of *blended learning*, I prefer to utilize the phrase *extended learning experience* when working with business leaders.

CLOs can use the Learning Capability Framework as a roadmap to enhance learning solutions and to build a true learning organization. Partnership with the business leaders relies upon a mutual understanding of the issues and the solutions, a shared language reflecting the strategic value of learning. The Learning Capability Framework illustrates and describes the multiple solutions available for both formal and self-directed enabling This common language and shared vision of a robust learning continuum supports the blending of multiple media and methods to achieve top individual and organizational performance.

Supercharge Your Blended Learning with Simulations

How do you craft an engaging classroom learning experience that will increase the retention of knowledge and maximize limited learning dollars? The key is to create a situation in the classroom that simulates a real-life experience.

The past few years have seen a strong movement toward blended learning curricula aimed at cost-effective skill building by employing a combination of e-Learning and classroom learning. Typically, organizations supplement classroom learning with e-Learning targeted at knowledge acquisition to create a baseline level of understanding before participants attend classroom programs. While the focus has been on developing these e-Learning capabilities, it is time to revisit how classroom learning is conducted to ensure that maximum benefits are realized.

With the wide acceptance of technology usage over the past 10 to 15 years, many classroom programs have evolved into presentation-based formats driven by PowerPoint® slides. Research has indicated that this is not the most effective way to learn, build skills or, more importantly, retain knowledge. The negative impact is even greater from a business perspective, due to the cost of bringing people into a central location to passively listen to presentations they most likely will not remember.

How do you craft an engaging classroom learning experience that will increase the retention of knowledge and maximize limited learning dollars? The key is to create a situation in the classroom that simulates a real-life experience.

Simulating reality provides a context for learners to retain the information and develop skills. It is similar to the apprenticeship employment model or on-the-job training. It is important to emphasize that simulations are not case studies. A case study encourages participants to take an external view to the problem by neatly summarizing salient information in a concise package. A simulation requires the participant to become intrinsically involved in the situation by completing a task or deliverable using data and inputs as they would appear in a real work environment. Developing this real-life context is a key to skill development and retention.

There are three primary design components to a classroom-based simulation: task, data, and time.

- **The TASK to be accomplished** – The first step is to identify the skills participants must develop during the program and then decompose those skills into specific tasks to be completed. The second step is to identify the data needed to support the completion of those tasks and the format that data is most likely to take (e-mail, system reports, articles, interviews).

- **The DATA to be analyzed** – Realistic data is the foundation of learning development during a simulation, because it requires participants to distill the relevant pieces of information from different sources and then interpret the data.

- **The TIME allowed to complete the TASK** – The third step is to evaluate whether there is enough data to support the task required in the allotted time. This component helps to create a realistic atmosphere by introducing enough time pressure to make the task manageable, yet challenging.

After the design phase, developing realistic data is critical to the effectiveness of the simulation and often consumes a significant portion of the development cycle. There are three approaches to data creation: dynamic, static and fabricated.

- **Dynamic Data** – This data is perhaps the easiest to develop because it requires participants to gather their own data. For example, participants asked to perform an external market analysis for a specific organization can turn to Internet or online resources and gather current market data.

- **Static Data** – This development involves gathering real-life data and "freezing" it at a point in time. For example, if the task is to revise the sales budget, the learning team would gather the data at a specific point in time, freeze it and then distribute the data during the learning session.

- **Fabricated Data** – This development is the most time-intensive and requires the most creativity and imagination because it requires the learning team to create an entire set of fictitious data to support each task. For example, if participants are asked to evaluate the organization's annual operational performance in the call center, the data required would involve fabricating call queue statistics, operational reports and so on.

Creating each piece of data is relatively straightforward. The challenge is to make sure the different data pieces are in sync and create the story with the problem areas you want participants to address.

There are many other design and development considerations that go into making a robust simulation that can withstand the scrutiny of business leaders and participants. These simulations can be created for individuals or teams, and can be scaled up to roll out to hundreds of participants simultaneously using a team-based format.

It is important to emphasize that the main objective of a learning event is to enhance employee performance. Simulations are the most effective means of developing employee skills that will be retained after the learning event and ultimately, enhance the overall performance of the business.

Leverage Knowledge Management to Create Learning

The most effective way to present a curriculum that leverages knowledge management in the enterprise is to give a visual representation in a curriculum map. A learning curriculum map provides all learners with relevant information, supplemental resources, job aids, knowledge objects, and learning objects to support their learning and certification needs.

The relationship between knowledge management and e-Learning has been frequently discussed. Although many of the concepts are highly interesting, learning professionals often ask the question: *How can the relationship between knowledge and e-Learning be leveraged to create learning?*

I believe that the main objective of knowledge management is to collect, store, disseminate and use knowledge throughout an enterprise. Knowledge objects can be documents, articles, PowerPoint® slides, audio files, websites and other sources of knowledge – typically made accessible to employees through a network and knowledge management portal. These knowledge objects are not developed to support a structured learning process but can be used as important source material for the design of a learning program. In addition, a selected number of knowledge objects can be integrated in a learning curriculum as supporting information, without converting each document or PowerPoint® deck into an *e-Learning page turner*, a type of e-Learning that does not contribute value to the learning process.

The most effective way to present a curriculum that leverages knowledge management in the enterprise is to give a visual representation in a *curriculum map*. A learning curriculum map provides all learners with relevant information, supplemental resources, job aids, knowledge objects, and learning objects to support their learning and certification needs. Below, the Enterprise Lean/Six Sigma Program (EL/SS), gives an example of this type of map. This online program provides learners with the opportunity achieve an industry-accepted Six Sigma certification. Based on professional experience and completion of this EL/SS curriculum, certification can be attained at a Green Belt, Black Belt, or Master Black Belt level.

The knowledge and learning objects are organized by topics, for example, Six Sigma and Enterprise Lean, and by sequential skill levels, including Basic, Advanced and Mastery.

The knowledge and learning objects include: e-Learning (self-paced e-Learning and recorded virtual classroom sessions), online books, PowerPoint® slides and online testing.

Example of a Curriculum Map: Enterprise Lean/Six Sigma

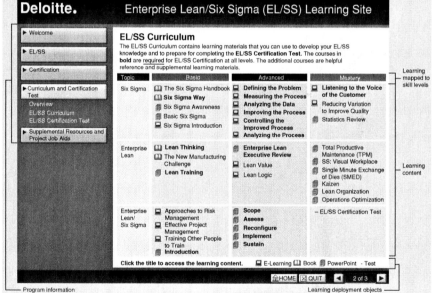

Benefits of the curriculum map concept include:

- An integrated learning approach using both knowledge and learning objects.
- All learning activities tracked/reported into a Learning Management System.

- User friendly interface and easy navigation.
- Designed for learning purposes.

From a business perspective, it reduces the time-to-market for knowledge and the development of skills globally and results in significant cost avoidance compared with the development and delivery of a completely classroom based program.

e-Learning By Design

Companies need to take a hard look at their overall learning curriculum and approach and deliberately select the use of all the appropriate facets of the blended model to create a total learning environment – converting classroom content to e-Learning where it makes sense, redesigning classroom experiences for high impact when face-to-face interactions are essential, and ensuring that the online learning experience is dynamic, engaging and fun.

It is a real page-turner. . . usually describes an exciting, dynamic *who-done-it* novel that keeps you engaged from the first moment right up to the last page. However, much of e-Learning *page-turning* has been exactly the opposite. Quick, inexpensive, low-level, online learning design in the advent of e-Learning produced *e-reading page-turners* – documents that were read online, with no interaction, no self-pacing, no dynamic exchanges – and learners engaged in this type of e-Learning have been disappointed.

The key questions in the minds of these learners and in the minds of their learning leaders were:

Is this learning? And: *Is all content delivered online, e-Learning?*

In finding answers to these questions, understanding the learner's motivation is a key. There are essentially two motivations to learn. In the first instance, the learner is motivated to acquire highly important knowledge and skills, when it is most needed. A person who has to complete their travel and expense report to be reimbursed for expenses incurred will be motivated to learn about the system, whether or not the content is presented in an engaging format. The second motivation to learn is that the learning process itself is engaging, accessible and fun.

Of course, excellent learning design ensures that both motivations are merged into a dynamic learning experience, combining the critical information needed with an application mastery process that transfers information into personal knowledge and ultimately – into individual change. However, it has long been recognized that supporting individual change requires on-going learning and application of this knowledge *over time*. Our experience has shown that the challenge of creating an extended learning continuum has been has been difficult to achieve when solely focused on one-time classroom events.

Using all of the potential learning media over the continuum of time, place, and interactions, is more powerful than a single classroom event. In a blended model for learning and growth, the learner is engaged through multiple inputs in their work and life, all of which enhance their performance and their ability to achieve the next level of competence.

The blended Learning and Growth Model, shown above, is based on research that has shown unequivocally that people learn most effectively while engaged in their job assignments. If you ask any CEO where they learned to do their job, they will cite the learning they experienced in a variety of job experiences. The multiple facets of the learning blended model, if deliberately focused on the learner's in-the-moment learning requirements, will result in high-impact performance improvement.

In this blended model, e-Learning offers a learning delivery methodology that enables and supports many aspects of the learning continuum, engaging the learner well beyond the classroom event in both time and place. It has the capacity to extend the learning through a variety of online *live* environments, such as, coaching, synchronous classrooms, and team chat rooms, and through limitless, self-directed learning, including, self-assessments, interactive e-courses, self-study guides, hot-links to further learning on related web-sites, and games.

As one aspect of a complete blended-model for growth and development, e-Learning now offers a rich resource of learning methodologies, supporting most learning styles and preferences – *e-reading* being just one of the various tools. However, e-Learning design excellence requires a deliberate, explicit choice of the right method for the level of learning desired. The Online Learning Continuum below indicates some possible applications of e-Learning methods that can best support each level of skill mastery.

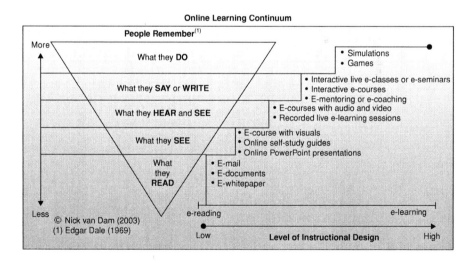

As you move along the continuum from e-reading to e-Learning, it is important to note that the degree of investment in instructional design increases the further out you move. An online business simulation is a powerful learning tool. However, it is one of the most expensive to develop in terms of design capability, time and resources.

Companies need to take a hard look at their overall learning curriculum and approach and deliberately select the use of all the appropriate facets of the blended model to create a total learning environment – converting classroom content to e-Learning where it makes sense, redesigning classroom experiences for high impact when face-to-face interactions are essential, and ensuring that the online learning experience is dynamic, engaging and fun.

Pioneers in any field have had experiences that enable those who follow to avoid their mistakes and build on the territory that they have explored. Thus, the quality of e-Learning has improved rapidly from the early experiences. There are better tools, a better understanding of learner's needs and expectations, and a directed focus on the design of the e-Learning experience. To support standards of excellence in e-Learning, ASTD has launched the ASTD Certification Institute, a certification program for e-Learning courseware. Courses submitted are evaluated against a set of rigorous standards developed by the ASTD Certification Commission. To learn more go to: www.ASTD.org.

Rather than believing that the technology of online learning alone is the answer, the new learning environment is, *by design*, a rich continuum, supporting learning from the beginner's awareness, all the way to mastery and individual performance improvement.

e-Learning Development at the Speed of Business

Rapid e-Learning development tools fill an important niche in e-Learning and are particularly powerful for infusing organizations with small, just-in-time learning objects.

E-Learning can deliver rapid time-to-market of new knowledge and skills and can be a key to successful, quick response to new business challenges. However, existing e-Learning development business models have proven to be time-consuming and inefficient to meet the demands of rapid execution.

Several rationales are given as reasons for this lag. Many argue that e-Learning development processes are not efficient, well-defined or optimized. Others argue that e-Learning courseware development is a function of art, creativity and science, and that therefore, it is not easy or desirable to standardize methods and processes. In addition, Elliott Masie has suggested that subject matter experts (SMEs) are the biggest drag on development of e-Learning, because of the conflicting demands for their time.

Thus, we must take a hard look at current e-Learning development models and identify areas for business process improvement. Efficiency improvements can be achieved if efforts are made to:

- Standardize development processes.
- Standardize approaches, including tools and templates.
- Define development approaches that satisfy different needs (i.e., virtual classroom, low versus high interaction).
- Reduce the number of development vendors.
- Leverage professional project management methods and tools.
- Assign SMEs who are committed, and communicate deliverable expectations.
- Use the right blend of onshore and offshore e-Learning development resources.

Companies also can improve the productivity of e-Learning development by using rapid e-Learning development tools. Rapid e-Learning tools provide a template-driven e-Learning development model that reduces development time from a few months to a few weeks or even days. Productivity gains can be achieved because programming time is eliminated. Although vendors suggest that anybody can use these rapid-development tools, learning functions must continue to engage professional instructional designers. In addition, it is necessary to ensure that proven methodologies are employed when developing learning.

Can rapid-development tools solve the SME time lag? Through the use of efficient data-collection tools, the proper training of instructional technologists as analysts, and the establishment of the appropriate rapport between the instructional technologist and the SME, the essential information can be collected in an efficient manner.

Although there is an important market for this segment of e-Learning courseware, learning leaders still must be explicit about the application of this approach. At the beginning of this century, early experiences with the page-turner type of e-Learning gave the e-Learning industry a bad name. Learners became disappointed in the quality of e-Learning as classroom programs were disbanded and replaced by PowerPoint® empowered by Flash®, with limited added value. Since then, the market of e-Learning solutions has developed from e-reading courseware to embrace the higher end of e-Learning applications that includes game- and simulation-based online courses.

However, rapid e-Learning development tools fill an important niche in e-Learning and are particularly powerful for infusing organizations with small, just-in-time learning objects. Do not think in terms of traditional e-Learning courses, which take at least an hour for completion. Rather, think in terms of short-burst access to knowledge that can support people's daily need for current information. Think of the more extensive e-Learning course as a novel, and sharable content objects as a series of 30-second commercials.

Learning is a professional business with drivers that enhance quality and productivity to support business goals. Therefore, it is important for learning executives to explore ways to optimize their e-Learning development business model and include *rapid development tools* as part of the development tool mix. At the same time, we need to ensure that we continue to strive to enhance the educational experience through high-quality e-Learning design.

e-Learning

Made in India

An increasing number of Fortune 500 companies such as IBM, Microsoft, GE, Motorola, and Deloitte, as well as medium and smaller organizations, outsource some of their e-Learning design and development to e-Learning companies based in India in order to save between 40 percent and 70 percent in e-Learning programming costs.

According to a survey of members of the Masie e-Learning Consortium, the development of a one-hour e-Learning program can cost enterprises between US\$3,000 (mostly *page-turners*) and US\$150,000 (higher end program or simulation).These numbers are consistent with other benchmarks done within the industry.

When reviewing estimates for e-Learning development, sometimes the focus is on the authoring and programming components of the development process, and not as much on the instructional design activities. Over the past years significant research has been conducted on the effectiveness of e-Learning. One of the key themes emerging from this research is that high quality, effective e-Learning should be based on learning theories grounded in research and developed using solid instructional design principles. It is for this reason that the design and development of world-class e-Learning requires significant investment.

Because most corporate universities do not have, or cannot hire, additional staff to develop company-specific e-Learning content, they reach out to external vendors to support this. An increasing number of Fortune 500 companies such as IBM, Microsoft, GE, Motorola, and Deloitte, as well as medium and smaller organizations, outsource their e-Learning design and development to e-Learning companies based in India in order to save between 40 percent and 70 percent in e-Learning programming costs.

Though a growing number of Indian firms offer e-Learning design and development capabilities, the results do not always live up to the promises, and there are number of reasons for this.

- **E-Learning design and development requires people with specific skills and capabilities.**
  Instructional design is a specialized discipline and you cannot expect a Flash® programmer to have mastered those skills. Some of the required instructional design capabilities include: conducting audience analyses, writing learning and performance objectives, structuring courses, designing and developing content, conceptualizing graphics, animations and interactivities, and creating assessments, as well as creating training manuals, lesson plans and learning presentations. E-Learning design and development is definitely a completely different profession than developing and applying software.

- **A number of e-Learning development firms in India have had very little experience in a variety of industries and topics.**
  There is not yet enough embedded experience in designing different learning solutions (such as simulations, assessments, and learning performance support) for different industries and on different subjects. As an example, there is a significant difference in designing a leadership program, a new hire orientation, or an e-Learning course to teach people how to use software or systems.

- **A number of e-Learning companies experience significant challenges from a development and delivery perspective.**
  The very nature of the business requires e-Learning content to be developed under a cohesive and shared environment, working with developers, writers, subject matter experts, project managers, programmers, and clients. E-Learning content has to be constantly shared, reviewed, critiqued, amended, and distributed. This collaborative challenge is compounded when all these people are located across different geographies and come from different backgrounds of expertise. Therefore, it is critical to have the following in place: proven e-Learning design methodologies and tools, distributed and collaborative development platforms, effective project management, and online workflow processes.

- **Effective project management of an offshore e-Learning development team is only possible with people who truly understand what it takes to design and develop e-Learning.** The quality of the e-Learning deliverables is highly correlated to the quality of input from the client. Therefore, the client's project management and involvement is critical to the success of the offshore development effort – it is a highly collaborative process.

The following provides a list of selection criteria for an offshore e-Learning development firm:

- Evidence of proven instructional design capabilities.
- Use of a proven e-Learning design and development methodology.
- Experience in developing different kinds of e-Learning solutions.
- Existence of industry expertise and experience with the development of industry-specific e-Learning courseware.
- Availability of technology systems and online workflow processes.
- e-Learning development from different locations with multiple team members.
- Transparency of development time for different deliverables.
- Language and cultural translation capabilities.
- At least 3 years of experience with e-Learning design and development.
- Certified e-Learning development processes in place (e.g., ISO9001).
- Embedded quality improvement approaches in place (e.g., Six Sigma).
- Existence of sustainable relationships with a number of key clients.

I believe there is a significant difference in firms who have made e-Learning design and development their core business, versus firms who have launched e-Learning capabilities as one of their services.

Needless to say, to make offshore e-Learning development a success, it is important to develop a long-term relationship with the vendor based on trust. There needs to be a desire on both sides of the relationship to work through potential challenges and to focus on ongoing process improvements to reach the ultimate goal of creating the highest quality e-Learning courseware.

The Business Results of Strategic New Hire On-Boarding

Why is onboarding important?

The absence of an intentional, strategic approach to new hire orientation is the black hole of organizational employee engagement and retention, with all of the related costs in low productivity and churn.

The Corporate Leadership Council's recent research demonstrates the real business impact of employee commitment: "Highly committed employees perform up to 20% better than less-engaged employees and are 87% less likely to leave the organization than employees with low levels of commitment" (Driving Performance and Retention Through Employee Engagement). Watson Wyatt's 2005 research found that organizations with high levels of employee commitment generated financial returns (in excess of the cost of capital investments) six times greater than those of companies with low employee commitment levels. The bottom line is that it is expensive to find, train, and replace employees. HR experts estimate that turnover costs from 30% to 50% of an employee's first year pay. Some suggest that the true cost is closer to 100%.

On the other hand, top performing companies have less than 5% of their employees leave during their first year. What are they doing differently? 75% of these companies have their new hires participate in a formal on-boarding process, spending more than 16 hours orienting their new hires. (TheBenchMarkPartners LLC)

What normally happens in new hire orientations?

In a Dilbert cartoon, new hire orientation is depicted as a process where the new hire is told to stand in a hallway and read several binders. This unfortunately reflects the experience of many. Typical onboarding in many enterprises includes: a company introduction, overview different policies and guidelines, how to use different information systems, exchanges of information from Human Resources, and so forth – a minimum investment of time and effort.

What drives this counterproductive organizational behavior?

There are several factors producing this result. There is little effort to ask new hires what their expectations are as they enter the organizations, their hopes, aspirations, and dreams. Also, time in the 21st century is probably our most limited resource, and committing the time for effective onboarding is difficult. The knowledge acquired during orientation is delivered too soon, and inefficiently applied much later at work. There is lack of consistency in the organizational messages. And, most orientation programs are not fun or exciting for the participants, or even for those responsible for the delivery.

Finally, and perhaps most importantly, it is not well understood that disengagement occurs during the first six months on the job. However, if the new hires believe that they have value to contribute to the organization, that their managers are committed to their success, and that their work has meaning and relevance to achieving organizational objectives, they become productive more quickly, and, as seen above, engaged employees produce six times the level of their disengaged colleagues.

What are the hallmarks of engaging new hire onboarding programs?

Best practices in orientation programs include most of the following:

- **Extending the onboarding program with multiple connections over time.**
  - The first experiences are targeted to understanding the organization, the people, the culture, mission, vision and values. Normally, this includes a welcome by leadership, an introduction to the work group, a tour of the workplace, and establishment of resources and space required to do the work.
  - Additional contacts are specific and intentional. The new hire is assigned a 'buddy' to turn to with questions and concerns.
  - Their manager creates a development plan for the new hire and meets several times during the first months to ensure that

performance expectations are understood, that the new hire is successful in integrating with the team and the work, and that they feel supported in accomplishing their goals.

- The most critical time for engagement is the first 90 days. It is during this time that the new hire is deciding whether they have made the right decision. Best practices both have milestones and measures during these months to ensure that the new hire has the experience necessary to ensure that they believe their choice was the correct one.

- **Including multiple resources and media to ensure that fun, just-in-time learning is available.**
  - Prior to arrival on the first day online learning provides a first glimpse of the organization, learning and growth opportunities, generating excitement and supporting the choice they have made.
  - E-enabled orientation includes: Online orientation schedules, materials, benefits and time report forms, online learning modules for the general company overview.
  - A variety of learning methods are employed, including: self paced e-learning, virtual classroom, process-embedded learning, classroom, and one-on-one coaching
  - Targeted learning is pushed out into their learning plan via the Learning Management System
  - Experiential and action learning are engaged to match the new generation expectations in collaboration and growth.

- **Building the relationships.**
  - The most effective person to convey the real and dynamic experience of working for the company is the recent, successful new hire. Engaging recent hires in the orientation, telling of their experiences is engaging and fun.
  - New careers thrive on networks. Build in intentional networking opportunities with the work team, colleagues across functions in the organization and leadership.

- **Keeping the future bright.**
  - Make sure that the view of the path and experience ahead are visible and that the connection to growth and development of a robust career are emphasized.

- Discuss future aspirations and sculpt job roles and responsibilities to ensure that the new hire is connected and engaged.

The loss to business in employee disengagement and turnover is compelling. Of course there are multiple perspectives on how these can be improved, and yet probably one of the easiest to fix and resolve is the employee onboarding process. Rather than being a period of uncertainty and boredom, it can be fun, interesting and exciting. By creating these positive emotions at the beginning of the company's relationship with the new hire, the new employee wants to deliver the best results and stay where they are appreciated, valued and productive.

Multi-Cultural Perspectives in Learning

It is only with the heart that one can see rightly; what is essential is invisible to the eye.

Antoine de Saint-Exupery

Developing Talent in China

One of key retention strategies that works especially well in China is providing Chinese employees and management with best-in-class learning and development opportunities. Ideally, the retention strategy links this growth and development with career development and performance management practices.

Despite a population of 1.3 billion, a growing number of global companies are experiencing significant challenges attracting and retaining talent in mainland China. Over the last decade measured by official GNP numbers, China's annual economic growth of approximately 9.5 percent has made the Chinese economy the 7th largest in the world, and many economists predict that the Chinese economy will outpace the US economy by 2020. China has actually doubled its GNP twice over the last twenty years. In comparison, it took the United States almost 50 years to do this.

The Chinese economy offers outstanding opportunities for US and European companies who want to tap into this huge domestic market. China has become the world's leading consumer. It leads the world in consumption of grain, meat, steel and other modern products, for example, cell phones. China has become the largest customer for Boeing's commercial aircrafts, and for Germany headquartered Volkswagen, China is their largest foreign market.

The growth of the economy has resulted in a booming demand for people in professional and managerial jobs including: business leaders, marketers, engineers, account managers, auditors, IT specialists, and human resources directors, among many others. McKinsey estimates that China will need to produce about 75,000 globally capable executives, over the next 5 years.

Most companies working in China try to close the talent-gap by:

- Sourcing Chinese candidates who have studied abroad (e.g., a large number of students from mainland China study in the USA and other countries).
- Expanding expatriate programs for experienced professionals. (Although, this is a relatively expensive option and will not be sufficient over time).
- Recruiting talent from the Chinese elite universities (e.g., Tsinghua University was the first university to launch an MBA program in 1991).
- Targeting people from other global Fortune 500 companies with experience.
- Acquiring local Chinese companies.

As demand for talent outstrips supply, employee turnover rates have jumped to over 30 percent in a number of companies. Additionally, compensation for professionals is increasing at a steady pace, closing the gap that formerly existed when compared to compensation in other Asian countries for experienced managers. Benefits are becoming a tool to help retention, again increasing the total cost to company. The shortage of talent is becoming a factor in the ability of global companies to meet their growth targets.

Instead of just focusing on recruiting and replacing talent, companies will need to pursue a strategy of employee retention initiatives. This is cost effective (the cost of a replacement can be 1.5–3 times annual salary) and will become a differentiator in attracting new talent. One of key retention strategies that works especially well in China is providing Chinese employees and management with best-in-class learning and development opportunities. Ideally, the retention strategy links this growth and development with career development and performance management practices.

This provides companies with a number of challenges including:

- *How to ensure that new hires are quickly assimilated within the enterprise?*
- *How to provide cost effective and efficient training?*
- *How to reach a dispersed workforce?*
- *How to provide training in Mandarin?*
- *How to address cultural differences in learning styles?*

A number of Fortune companies, including GE, Deloitte, L'Oreal, McDonalds, and Motorola, among others, have established Corporate Universities and leadership development programs in China, and have established partnerships with the top tier Chinese universities, also connecting with and leveraging international faculty. Important professional management competences that have been identified as critical for development include: risk and quality management, international management, working across cultures, entrepreneurship, project management, accounting, and sales and marketing, among others.

With such a vast demand and need to meet the learning and development requirements for the future, classroom-based programs alone won't be sufficient to embed all the necessary competences. E-Learning-based learning has experienced a fast adoption rate in a large number of companies in China. Overall, Internet usage has grown rapidly over recent years and a growing number of Chinese universities are offering students e-Learning courses.

A number of Chinese e-Learning companies have developed and localized cost effective e-Learning in Mandarin, driving a fast adoption for people who are less proficient in English or who prefer to learning in Mandarin. Although, connectivity and bandwidth can still be an issue, most Fortune companies can provide employees with high speed access to e-Learning in their offices.

The demand for growth in the pool of management and professional talent, the eagerness in China for learning and growth, and the exponential growth in e-Learning usage and access have generated a significant interest from both companies and universities in China to implement e-Learning strategies and blended leadership development programs. In addition, the experiences of companies and universities implementing e-Learning strategies in China will become instructive for all of us as we generate and support the development of China's management and professional human resource capabilities.

Learning Programs for Multiple Generations in the Workforce

Four generations work side by side in today's workforce. Veterans, Baby Boomers, Gen X and Gen Y, and each has different attitudes about their jobs, careers and learning.

It is important to remember that generation classifications are generalities and the lines between generations are not strict. Yet, research has shown that most groups can be characterized by a certain set of attitudes and beliefs. Today the generations in the workforce are:

- Veterans, born before 1946.
- Baby Boomers born from 1946–1964.
- Gen Xers born from 1965–1980.
- Gen Yers born after 1980.

Generational differences have real implications for how employers and employees work together. Each generation brings a different set of attitudes to the job. Research, in general, has shown that Baby Boomers put a heavy focus on work as an anchor in their lives while Gen Xers enjoy work, but are more concerned about work/life balance. Gen Yers often have different priorities. Because of their deep reliance on technology, they believe they can work flexibly anytime, anyplace and that they should be evaluated on work product – not on how, when or where they got it done. Surprisingly, they want long-term relationships with employers, but on their own terms. The *real revolution* is a decrease in career ambition in favor of family time, less travel and less personal pressure.

Gen Xers and Gen Yers are the first generations to grow up with computers and the Internet as part of their lives. Constant experience in the networked world has had a profound impact on their approach to problem-solving and collaboration. While Baby Boomers see video games as diversions or toys, for Gen Xers and Gen Yers they are something distinctly different. The next generation of workers is coming into the workforce with skills that their elders never could have imagined.

Experience with interactive media such as instant messaging, text messaging, blogs and especially multi-player games allows many young people to develop new skills, new assumptions and new expectations about their employers. Current research suggest, for example that gaming can be an excellent preparation for business. Serious gamers are likely to be: more skilled and multi-tasking, agile in making decisions, evaluating risks and managing dilemmas, flexible and persistent in the face of change, and highly skilled in social networking and team activities.

Won't the new generation adapt to current business realities?
Certainly they will, to an extent. But two facts are very different today compared to when the Baby Boomers entered the workforce 30+ years ago, or the Gen Xers some 15–20 years ago. First, demographics – the law of supply and demand is at work. That is, there are fewer Gen Yers than Baby Boomers at the time of initial entry into the workplace, therefore, the probability of Gen Yers getting a lot more of what they want is much higher than for previous generations. Secondly, technology – the technology now exists to support the Gen Y preference to work more flexibly and virtually, and this capacity to work anyplace at anytime simply did not exist until very recently.

What can we learn from Gen Yers?
The Gen Yers are coming into the workforce with networking, multiprocessing, and global-mindedness skills that older generations can learn from. In addition, Gen Yers are technology natives who can drive a role reversal by mentoring technology-challenged Baby Boomers. And finally, maybe all can learn something useful from the Gen Y (and Gen X) focus on working more flexibly with a more dual-centric focus on both work and family.

Why should a business leader care what Gen Yers think: they're young and likely will change their minds anyway?
It is true that young people change their minds often. However, during this formative period of their teens, young people are making major decisions as to which college to attend and what to major in. Given

young people's profound skepticism of large businesses, in particular, it is quite likely that many will not be attracted to fields of study found attractive in prior generations, or may present significant on-boarding challenges for enterprises.

What are the implications for Learning?
Gen Yers can learn from facilitated sharing of knowledge in a typical classroom environment. Yet, Gen Yers prefer to learn in networks or teams, using multi-media and expect to be entertained and excited during the learning intervention. Experiential learning is important for them. Therefore, it is the expectation that business simulations will become the next wave of games which can help familiarize young people with a business previously unknown to them. Simulations also offer the opportunity to track skill development and open a new source of talent tracking and recruitment.

Crafting a Multi-Cultural e-Learning Strategy

In the past, learners were brought out of their own environment to experience learning in a different place, perhaps even a different country. A critical aspect of e-Learning implementation is that the learner remains very much in their own culture when engaged in the learning, with local cultural cues in full force around them.

Innovations in technology and increasing global access to the Internet are pushing relentlessly toward a seamless world online. A host of opportunities, including e-Learning, are becoming available in regions where lack of access has hindered growth in the past. Yet, as Geert Hofstede stated so well: *"The export of ideas to people in other countries without regard for the values context in which these ideas were developed – can be observed in the domains of education, and in particular, management and organization"*. *(Culture and Organizations: Software of the Mind)*

As we look at the global expansion of the Internet and the experiences of new global regions interacting in the eWorld, we find other dimensions are at play in speedy adoption of e-Learning. To be successful in launching an e-Learning initiative, four important technology pillars must be in place: competitive drivers, information technology infrastructure, regional/national laws and investments, and high quality courseware. In addition, the cultural drivers of individuals and groups play a critical role and when understood can form the capstone for the adaptation of e-Learning development and usage in various geographic areas.

This perspective and related challenges pose important questions: *What are the four pillars to successful e-Learning implementation? What is the definition of culture?* And: *What is required to deliver culturally adaptive e-Learning?*

The Platform for e-Learning: The Four Pillars

- **Pillar One – Competitive Drivers**

  e-Learning can support globalization. However, the drivers must be identified and a clear business case developed that supports launching e-Learning in new geographies, which can include for example: clear ROI, projected cost savings in decreased travel and facility costs, demand for rapid, just-in-time, distributed skill development, global deployment of learning, and employee retention.

- **Pillar Two – Information Technology Infrastructure**

  Attention must be paid to hardware, software and bandwidth.
  - Hardware

    Several multinational companies have given their employees PC's to have in their home, to increase capacity for global electronic communications, including e-Learning.
  - Software

    Media players must be used for most engaging materials. However in some Asian countries, high level security hinders individuals from downloading applets without obtaining administrative permission.
  - Bandwidth

    In 2006, about 190M people globally enjoy high speed broad band connections globally. South Korea and the Netherlands have the highest % of population using high speed Internet connections. Although high speed Internet connections keep growing fast – a lot of countries are just at a very early stage of adoption. For example not more than 1.6 percent of the population of Brazil had access to high speed Internet in 2006. In Africa and in the Middle East, less than 10 percent of the people use the Internet.

- **Pillar Three – Regional/National Laws and Investments**

  Investment and Policy initiatives can make an enormous difference in the national penetration of e-Learning adoption. However, in some cases existing laws have unintended consequences.

- Privacy
  - Unions in Europe are very apprehensive about accessible data, e.g. results of an assessment or test being transported to a Learning Management System. For example, a European country may have excellent Internet access, but names and test scores are not transmitted over the Internet because of the *safe harbor* regulations.
- Pipeline Access
  - France has worked to receive flat rate Asymmetric Digital Subscriber Line (ADSL) with a related increase in Net access and home PC sales.
  - In Italy, government initiatives allowed citizens to deduct the cost of Net access and phone charges from their taxes, resulting in millions of citizens being connected.
- Investments
  - The European Community has published a commitment from all the member countries to equip every citizen with the skills needed to live and work in the information society, providing a European diploma for basic IT skills, including a decentralized certification procedure.

- **Pillar Four – High Quality Courseware**
  Learning must be engaging, motivational and fun.

- Early television shows were basically radio programs broadcast in a new format – people standing in place and reading scripts. Similarly, early e-Learning courses were essentially PowerPoint® slides with forward and back buttons. Now capability has been enhanced by new media, producing blended courses with simulations, games, and synchronous learning.

The Development of an e-Learning Culture

There must also be serious consideration to the development of an appropriate e-Learning culture. Culture is defined as *a shared set of learned assumptions, values and behavior developed over time, which influence thoughts, feelings and day-to-day actions. The core of culture is formed by values.* These are among the first things children learn, usually embedded by the age of 10, and after that time difficult to change.

Geert Hofstede has identified and researched four dimensions of culture that can have a significant bearing on adoption of new approaches, and these are depicted in the graphic below, including: uncertainty avoidance, power distance, individualism, and work/life balance. These dimensions of difference can point to explicit design elements and actions which may speed the adoption of e-Learning, which are described in the following grid.

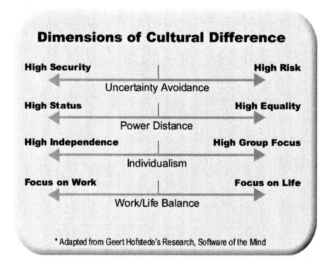

Dimensions of Cultural Difference

Dimension	Description	Potential Impact on e-Learning
Uncertainty Avoidance	**Security versus Risk.** Indicates the degree to which one is comfortable with ambiguous situations and can tolerate uncertainty. High security cultures prefer formal rules.	The unproven field of e-Learning can be seen in a High Risk country as fun, motivational, interesting, but can be seen in a High Security country as dangerous and risky.

Power Distance	**Status versus Equality.** A measure of the inequality between bosses and inferiors, and the extent to which this is accepted. High Status countries are much more comfortable with a larger differential than High Equality cultures.	In a High Equality country, the equality between superiors and workers implies a feeling of knowledge being shared by all. In a High Status country, status differences require a *'sage on the stage'* to teach what needs to be known.
Individualism	**Independence versus Group.** The degree to which one thinks in terms of 'I' versus 'We'. Either ties between individuals are loose, or people are part of a cohesive group throughout their lives.	In High Independence countries, there is a sense of 'being in the driver's seat' of your career and work choices. In a High Group country, the success of the group is paramount.
Work/Life Balance	**Focus on Work versus Focus on Life.** The degree to which achievement and success are more valued than caring for others and the quality of life. This dimension is also described as the relative masculine and feminine influences in the workplace.	People 'live to work', or 'work to live'. High Work Focus countries require recognition, sense of achievement, and certification. In a High Life Focus country, work related issues, including learning, would need to be managed within the context of the work day.

The ideal e-Learning Culture Print* of a society that would readily adapt e-Learning may be that of the United States.

---

* (Footnote: All data for the Culture Print graphics included in this article are adapted from Geert Hofstede, *Cultures and Organizations: Software of the Mind,* McGraw-Hill 1997).

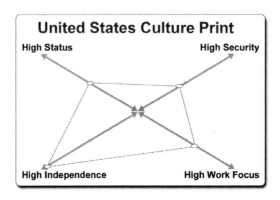

Dimension	Impact
Mid-Range in Equality/Status	Accept content in learning not necessarily promoted or presented by a recognized expert or teacher, but also enjoy recognition for accomplishment.
High in Independence	Able to enjoy the independence of tailoring their 'MyLearning' portfolio, and pursuing their own path. Sense of career ownership drives interest in acquiring new skills.
High in Risk	Capable of taking risks in exploring something not completely proven, learning in E-Learning time and space.
Mid-Range in Achievement	Equally focused on work and life, able to both accept e-Learning opportunities at work, but also will engage anytime/anywhere.

Americans adopted e-Learning more quickly because self-directed, personalized, on-demand, specific, peer-to-peer learning meets many of the cultural drivers already in place.

However, the verbatim export of the above approach to e-Learning adoption may not work in every culture. The challenge in fostering global e-Learning adaptation is to effectively integrate the new learning approach into the embedded cultural values of the country.

A view of a Culture Print for four other countries offers a perspective snapshot of how e-Learning methods, content, and approaches may be *'localized'* more effectively to engage the learner in an experience that recognizes and leverages their cultural drivers.

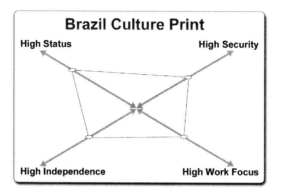

Brazil   **Selected Recommendations for e-Learning Initiatives**

High Status
Include the supervisor in the directions to engage in
e-Learning, reward completion, and involve known subject
matter experts visibly in presentations during online
Synchronous sessions or in Flash® content.

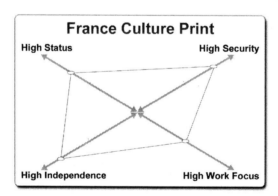

France   **Selected Recommendations for e-Learning Initiatives**

High Independence & High Status
Use features such as 'MyLearning' to enable workers to create
and pursue their own learning pathways, while including the
supervisor visibly in the promotion of e-Learning initiatives.

High Security
Provide small early 'wins' in the e-Learning experience to
develop acceptance and familiarity with the tools and
approach. Ensure success through coaching and monitoring.

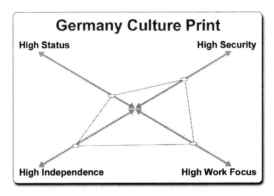

| Germany | **Selected Recommendations for e-Learning Initiatives** |

High Equality
Share access and network knowledge across the organization through e-Learning communities, using e-Learning to foster exchanges of 'best practice'.

High Independence
Provide universal access and linkages to multiple sources of e-Learning opportunity.

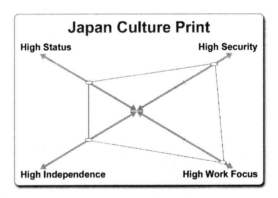

| Japan | **Selected Recommendations for e-Learning Initiatives** |

High Work Focus
Assign individual roles of leadership periodically within the group e-Learning experience, where personal expertise is given an opportunity to be observed and commended. Assessments and certification may also contribute to the sense of achievement.

"The best globalized website doesn't hint that it has been translated or localized at all. Rather, it's transparent in the look and feel as if it were originally written and designed in and for the target language and culture." Barry Parr, Director, IDC e-Learning and eCommerce Strategies Research. Recognition of cultural drivers and the global trends in e-Learning growth cited earlier have led to the rapid expansion of a new industry *localization* – the translation and tailoring of e-Learning content. Localization companies translate not just the language, but the whole look and feel of the material and experience, making people feel the material is written for them.

In the past, learners were brought out of their own environment to experience learning in a different place, perhaps even a different country. A critical aspect of e-Learning implementation is that the learner remains very much in their own culture when engaged in the learning, with local cultural cues in full force around them. Microcultural issues that can be ignored when bringing learners out of their normal day-to-day life, must be embraced when pushing learning out through the e-Learning to the learner, who is sitting in their own office or home in Oslo, Osaka, Sao Paulo, Frankfurt or Beijing.

Within the blended model of e-Learning, there are significant opportunities to address these cultural dimensions, deliberately and effectively. The five considerations that should top your list as you move into a globalized e-Learning strategy include:

- Ensure that the *Four Platform Pillars for e-Learning* are solidly in place.
- Review the *Culture Print* for each country prior to a rollout of e-Learning.
- Conduct your own *Organization Cultural Assessment* to identify significant factors at play.
- Select and implement e-Learning initiatives that link to *Cultural Drivers*.
- *Measure e-Learning* effectiveness and manage continuous improvements.

Leveraging the Business Impact of Learning

People are definitely a company's greatest asset. It doesn't make any difference whether the product is cars or cosmetics. A company is only as good as the people it keeps.

Mary Kay Ash

The Emerging Role of the Chief Learning Officer

Maximizing the capacity of each individual through targeted learning and development over time and space is crucial to excellence and this defines the role of the CLO. With a seat at the strategy table, there is a requirement that learning creation and execution are linked specifically and intentionally to the business goals of the organization, and that the language of business is spoken.

The challenges are mounting for the Chief Learning Officer (CLO) as they work strategically to support success for their companies and people.

The upcoming retirement of the generation of baby boomers will bring significant knowledge gaps in organizations, and the entering generation of employees has a very different learning style, more technology-enabled and team-oriented than previous generations. Most enterprises will expect people to develop new competences at a faster pace than ever before, as product life cycles are getting shorter, and organizations are becoming flatter, more knowledge-driven, complex and global.

Executives in all industries are seeking to leverage the untapped talent of their people, and they are turning to the CLO to ensure that this talent is energized and engaged through sophisticated, advanced learning systems and approaches. No longer on automatic pilot, it is not enough to engage in delivering traditional classroom learning in isolation. Too much is at stake and the 21st century offers exceptional opportunities to deliver learning through cutting-edge channels, resources and tools. Learning must be integrated into the execution of strategy, developed collaboratively, extended through both time and geographies in a rapid, seamless execution, and must demonstrate valuable bottom-line results.

A new CLO role has emerged and involves strategic performance in a number of significant areas including:

Establishing Learning Governance Structure.
It is critical to engage business leaders and Information Technology, Human Resource and Learning leaders to develop and shape a vision for learning and jointly make decisions. This support will optimize the implementation and adoption of new initiatives in today's complex enterprises.

Building an Employer Brand through Investments in Learning.
A company brand is one of the most import assets of an organization. Investments in people learning and development can help to enhance the employer brand, and position the organization as an *Employer of Choice*. The CLO must to play an active role in making this a reality.

Integrating Learning with Performance Management Practices.
Performance management has emerged as strong area of focus for most enterprises. The Learning function must be involved in a number of areas including: developing competency frameworks, mapping courses to competences, and the design of individual knowledge assessments. This enables employees to build their personal learning plans and keep track of learning completions, gaining certifications, and building critical competencies in their desired career path.

Creating and Supporting an Enterprise-Wide Learning and Collaboration Platform.
An enterprise-wide learning and collaboration platform provides the foundation for access to knowledge and learning, the capacity to track and report learning activities, and the opportunity for people to share knowledge through communities of practice and expert networks.

Providing Decentralized Capabilities to Create and Share Knowledge.
Previously, learning programs were for the most part centrally developed and delivered to people throughout the organization. In today's world, it is expected that information and knowledge flows through the entire enterprise bottom-up, horizontally, and top-down. Universal access to the tools and applications that enable distribution of knowl-

edge and sharing of expertise within the organization is mandatory. Examples of these technology supported tools include: collaboration platforms, virtual classrooms, and rapid e-Learning development platforms, among others.

Designing Blended Learning Solutions.

New learning solution designs provide people with the most efficient and effective way to acquire and share knowledge and develop skills. True blended learning solutions include one or more of the following components: classroom, online learning, coaching and mentoring, online referenceware, communities of practice, expert networks and information repositories.

Developing the Value Proposition and Measurement of Learning.

Enhancing learning capabilities requires significant investments which can only be approved if a sound business case is communicated. In order to retain investment levels year-over-year, it is important to show the business impact that investments have achieved in enabling the talent to perform effectively and efficiently to achieve strategic goals.

The good news is that the CLO can leverage and blend a broad portfolio of learning methods and tools to support business and people development including:

- Classroom programs – facilitated sessions, classroom simulations, workshops, and seminars.
- Self-paced e-Learning courses and live virtual classroom sessions.
- Podcasts, webinars and TVonline.
- PDA and mobile-based learning.
- Online job aids and performance support tools.
- Process Embedded Learning
- Online books and executive summaries.
- Access to rich knowledge repositories.
- Coaching and mentoring (both live and online).
- Communities-of-Practice.
- Expert networks.
- Online skill and competency assessments and feedback tools.
- Learning and career development planning tools.

The primary resource to be engaged in the execution of strategy is the skills, knowledge and energy of the people. Maximizing the capacity of each individual through targeted learning and development over time and space is crucial to excellence and this defines the new role of the CLO. With a seat at the strategy table, there is a requirement that learning creation and execution are linked specifically and intentionally to the business goals of the organization, and that the CLO speaks the language of business.

Effective Learning Governance Drives Business Results

The answer to the learning centralization/decentralization challenge lies in establishing a governance structure of learning councils that provide cross-enterprise oversight of important initiatives in a decentralized model.

The tension between a centralized learning function and the needs of individual countries and business lines has been a source of wide swings in the organization of the Learning function over the years.

Currently forward-looking enterprises are realizing a strong return on centralizing shared learning services, leadership development, and learning design and development. This growing number of firms are centralizing learning capabilities and building shared service centers to enhance their learning efficiency and effectiveness. According to a 2005 study from Bersin & Associates, areas where shared services in learning have the most positive business impact include: learning management system administration, e-Learning content development and integration, learning architecture, performance consulting, results measurement, and new-hire orientation. Key business drivers for the development of shared learning services are to:

- Avoid redundant systems and resources.
- Leverage the use of specialists, benefit from economies of scale.
- Gain brand and quality compliance of courseware.
- Maximize the use of outsourcing and off-shoring.

Leadership development is also centralized in most enterprises. Uniform competency frameworks ensure that learning interventions can be designed to support new-skills development and reinforce specific leadership behaviors that need to be consistent throughout the enterprise in order to embed the organizational cultural values and drive innovation, change and results.

However learning budgets are more difficult to centralize for a variety of reasons. A significant number of learning initiatives are still developed and deployed on a more decentralized basis. In this decentralized organizational model, similar learning programs might be developed in different units, resulting in inconsistent knowledge transfer and inefficient use of valuable resources.

For this reason, some organizations are centralizing all learning budgets. However, this can be hard to achieve for a variety of reasons:

- Learning investments typically follow a Profit & Loss structure. Allocating the dollars separate from this framework could result in a disconnect between the business, which is responsible for results, and human capital development.
- The allocation of a centralized learning budget can be complex and time-consuming, posing a challenge to the need for fast-changing skill development in different business units and geographies.
- A centralized budget might be under constant scrutiny for cost savings when the overall enterprise is looking for measures to show more profitability.

The answer to this centralization/decentralization challenge lies in establishing a governance structure of learning councils that provide cross-enterprise oversight of important initiatives in a decentralized model. Some areas that must be taken into consideration in the establishment of learning councils include:

- **The creation of a number of learning governance councils.**
  Different learning activities require the engagement of people with distinctive skills and roles. Examples might include a leadership development council, a learning technology council and councils for global business units. Leaders of these different councils should be represented in an overall global learning council.

- **The development of clear, strategic objectives.**
  Specific objectives must be set at the enterprise level to provide direction. For example, one objective could be cost-effective and high-quality learning content that supports the business model and strategy for the future.

- **The definition of the scope.**
  The scope of a learning council can be defined as narrow or broad. Examples of scope could include making recommendations in strategic areas of investment and priorities with respect to leadership development, sharing and communicating best learning practices, and reviewing and managing vendor relationships.

- **The determination of the operating principles.**
  Clarity is required in a number of areas. For example: *Which roles should be represented in the learning council? How frequently will different councils meet? What is the best reporting line for the councils? How are decisions to be made?*

In our global, diversified, complex, networked organizations, it is definitely possible and assuredly most desirable to increase efficiency and effectiveness within the Learning function by implementing a governance model that is aligned with the business. The learning governance council structure leverages competencies, insights and impact across enterprise boundaries, while retaining the maximum responsiveness to diverse geographic, business unit and cultural realities and requirements.

The Return to a Centralized Learning Function

As multinationals move toward global integration to serve customers, they are also competing for talent and leadership on a global basis. This requires a new approach to business strategy and strategy execution, with a closely related impact on learning strategy.

Many have offered creative approaches to the design of organizational structures for the Learning function. Leaders and authors agree that there is no best practice. However, it is widely accepted that *structure* should align with and support the *business strategy*.

Learning functions in multinational organizations have to a large extent been decentralized in the organization. The strategy reflected the desire to stay very close to the customers of the learning programs and to provide training programs targeted to the unique needs of the learners. As a result, most international enterprises support a number of internal training organizations, organized by business unit, country and geographic region. Additionally, learning organizations are segmented by the target audience they support, for example: Information Technology Group, Sales, or Leadership. Recently, I learned from one multinational that they had more than 40 different education functions acting autonomously.

Until now, little to zero financial information has been available within multinationals regarding overall investments in learning and training, and the effectiveness of learning for the enterprise. Additionally, there are significant overlaps and redundancies in the courseware and curricula developed and delivered through so many different training groups.

However, as multinationals move toward global integration to serve customers, they are also competing for talent and leadership on a global basis. This requires a new approach to business strategy and strategy execution, with a closely related impact on learning strategy.

Some strategic business drivers which have an impact on learning include:

- Decrease time to market for new products and services globally.
- Increase speed of implementation of new business models/processes and technologies.
- Retain customers worldwide.
- Attract, develop and retain leadership.
- Improve innovation and drive change through the organization.
- Enhance the productivity of the workforce.
- Engage and retain of talent.

Due to the fast emergence of e-Learning and learning management systems (LMS), enterprises are now able to take a more strategic look at learning and align learning more closely with these strategic business goals and outcomes. Global enterprises can make learning available throughout their entire enterprise by using learning management systems combined with targeted e-Learning – mapping learning to competency models, and tracking usage, completions and business impact.

Obviously, these efficiencies are adversely impacted if a variety of LMS systems or different LMS instances are implemented within various countries, business units and/or departments. The opportunity costs and the real costs accrued due to lack of integration and duplication of effort in the maintenance and support of multiple systems and initiatives are readily recognized. Additionally, there are redundancies in system configuration, system administration and updates, while at the same time there is a lack of insight on the overall development of competencies within the enterprise and little ability to aggregate enterprise-wide information on investments in learning.

On the other hand, significant economies of scale are realized by having a centralized LMS support group versus building and replicating these capabilities in different business units and countries. Particularly, if one takes into consideration that much of the required centralized support can be completed in countries with lower wages. (A growing number of Fortune companies have established *blended* offshore teams to support this).

The same applies for the development of e-Learning courseware. Learning needs analysis must be done by people who work closely with business unit or country leadership and subject matter experts.

However, it is very inefficient and ineffective to establish relationships with a large number of vendors in different countries on content that is globally required. Costs to consider include:

- Time involved in multiple Request For Proposal processes.
- Similar, perhaps competing, processes within the IT and legal departments to provide vendors access to company infrastructure and security.
- Educating multiple vendors on company specific policies and procedures.

The attached table provides a brief summary on activities which the learning organization could consider in the decision whether to centralize or decentralize learning investments and initiatives.

ACTIVITY	CENTRALIZED	DECENTRALIZED
Learning Governance	✓	
Learning Strategy	✓	
Training/Learning Needs Analyses	✓	✓
Curriculum Development	For Global curricula	For Country or Business Unit specific curricula
Global Vendor Contracts	✓	
Usage of Subject Matter Expertise		✓
Classroom Program Development	✓	Localization
e-Learning Course Design & Development	✓	Localization

LMS/Learning Portal System Administration, Management & Support	✓	
Certification and Staffing of Trainers/Lecturers	✓(Certification)	✓(Staffing)
Communication & Marketing of Learning Solutions	✓	✓

Why Marketing of Learning Matters

The CLO is running a business with all the dimensions and demands incumbent upon a business executive including the integration of marketing and sales.

Significant investments are made by enterprises in the marketing and sales of their products and services. This can easily range from 10 – 50 percent of their total costs. This is very different when you look at the average budget of the corporate Learning function. Typically, Learning functions spend significant percentages of their budget in product (course) development or acquisition, but assume that *'if they build it, they will come'* and that their customers (employees) will come and buy. Therefore, their investments in marketing and sales are almost non-existent.

This was not that problematic until a few years ago because the product portfolio (learning curriculum) was limited to a number of classroom programs and most employees knew what was available. Furthermore, learning customers were asked (or better told) to attend the classroom programs by their management and therefore there was no need for the corporate learning function to play a more proactive role in the marketing and promotion of the learning programs.

This has changed significantly since the introduction of e-Learning, whereby most learning curricula have expanded from approximately 50 courses to 1,500+ courses. As a result customers need better information regarding the learning programs available and how they can benefit from engaging in the opportunity. Furthermore, recent research has confirmed that marketing is one of the key critical organizational capabilities for making e-Learning successful in companies.

There are number of other business drivers for establishing strong marketing capabilities within corporate Learning functions/ universities. First, Learning functions do best when they regard their employees as their customers. Customers always have a choice of what and where they buy. In the 21st century, the importance of staying at the cutting-edge of individual professional capabilities is so critical, that if employees are not happy with the learning and development capabilities provided by their current employer's learning function, they may move on to another company that can provide better learning opportunities.

Secondly, the Chief Learning Officer must be able to create value for the stakeholders – this includes valuable skill building for the customers (employees), but also a value proposition for the investors and stakeholders in the enterprise (leadership and shareholders) that the learning capabilities provided develop critical skills in a very effective and efficient matter. In other words – the CLO is running a business with all the dimensions and demands incumbent upon a business executive, including the integration of marketing and sales.

I had the opportunity to be the judge for the CUX (Corporate University) Exchange) Best Practices Award for Marketing Learning. Over the past years, a number of corporate universities have made significant progress in developing and launching internal marketing capabilities. Some of the best practices in the marketing of learning included:

- **Brand the Corporate Learning Function or Corporate University.**
  One of the most valuable assets of companies is their brand. Similarly, for employees around the world it is important that the learning activities are recognized. Therefore, many enterprises have launched a *'brand-name'* for their corporate university or learning function.

- **Maintain a Dynamic Learning Portal Management.**
  Very successful commercial websites and portals are designed from a user-friendly graphical and navigation perspective. More importantly, content on portals must change frequently if one expects the learner to return to the learning portal. This requires active learning content management and learning portal management.

- **Provide Personalized Marketing.**
  Companies have very diverse customers with very specific needs. Therefore, it is not good practice to overload all people with messages on new learning programs which might not be applicable to them. Personalized marketing strategies, that provide information based on an individual's profile, push out *learning alerts* based on employee requirements or on their subscription to specific alerts. A

number of Learning Management Systems provide a user interface that is similar to the Amazon online bookstore experience.

- **Leverage Established Learning Brands.**
  Most names of learning vendors are not recognized by people. However, using established education brands means a lot for people. For example, a number of learning functions have used the Harvard Business School Publishing suite of online programs very successfully for the promotion of e-Learning leadership courseware.

- **Market Learning Solutions versus Products.**
  Employees are not necessarily engaged and excited if we promote a product called *101 – Marketing*. Packaging and marketing of learning products as solutions provide more value for the people for example:

Learning Solution	Cost	Results
• Negotiation for Results	2 hours of your time	Creative and winning negotiation skills.
• Presentation Development	4 hours of your time	Clear, effective presentations and messages.
• Project Management Certification	20 hours of your time	Strong Project Management skills which are externally recognized.

Other Examples of Successful Marketing Strategies include:
- Online Learning Newsletters using a variety of templates.
- Posters to support learning programs and solutions.
- Including learning as part of other initiatives.
- Engaging countries and learners in marketing campaign.
- Customer relationship management and customer intelligence.
- Marketing metrics for measuring progress.

Finally, in order to successfully market and promote learning initiatives, the CLO working with the Learning function needs to employ marketing professionals who can work with the entire learning team to develop and execute a strategic marketing plan.

Learning Economics

Why Training Spending Levels Don't Matter Anymore

At a minimum, it is compelling for each individual enterprise to measure more than the simplistic data offered by overall learning investment and the number of training hours. More important is the measurement of the contribution learning is making to the achievement of strategic performance, leveraging efficiencies offered by 21st century Internet-based learning capabilities, and contributing to the creation of shareholder value.

Recently, I reviewed the 2006 list of the Training Top 100* companies to explore the best practices and current trends in learning.

Companies that entered submissions to be considered for the Training Top 100 answered multiple questions. One important question asked for the assessment of *Training Budget as % of Payroll* (as an input variable) and another asked for the *Average Annual Number of Training Hours per Person* (an output variable). This set of questions recognizes that organizations still use *investment levels* and *training hours* as benchmark data to make the business case within their organization for more dollars and to drive for more learning hours for their workforce.

Everybody will agree that if you don't spend any dollars in learning that the average number of learning hours will be zero. Furthermore, if you invest significantly in learning, it is likely that the number of learning hours will be high too. If one would assume a linear relationship between those variables, you would get a 45 degree line as depicted in the graph below that compares *Learning Investment Levels* and average number of *Training Hours*.

* Information from Training Top 100, Training Magazine

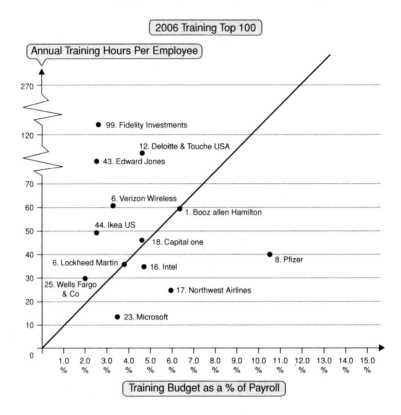

I have included in the visual the names of selected companies on the 2006 Training Top 100 list with their ranked number on the list prior to their name.

(Note: *Not all companies submitted Training Investments as % of Payroll, and I selected only a few that did to include in the visual. The source for the data is the Training Top 100 publication and the data was provided by the companies who submitted an application.*)

This comparison leads to interesting observations:

- There is a wide distribution on both spending levels and on the average number of learning hours.
- There are companies with relatively low spending levels who provide their people with a relatively high number of learning hours (and vice versa).
- There are companies who have the same level investment but with very different output in terms of number of learning hours.

- From the comparative data, it is unclear if *High Learning Investments* and/or a *High Number of Learning Hours* lead to a higher ranking on the Training Top 100.

Economists typically may look at ways to explain this by looking at efficiency and effectiveness.

From an **efficiency** perspective, one can say that there are companies who seem to be able to do more with their dollars than others. This might have been due to their ability to:

- Reduce indirect and administrative (transactional) learning costs.
- Automate most learning business processes (e.g. training needs analyses, courses registration, approvals, evaluations, distribution of training material).
- Outsource and/or offshore learning capabilities.
- Centralize learning capabilities to avoid overlap.
- Move towards an e-Learning delivery model which provides significantly increased learning hours for less cost than classroom training.

Another approach to clarify the variances in spending levels and total number of learning hours is to look at the **effectiveness** of the learning and ask:

- *Did the learning investments build critical capabilities needed for the business?*
- *Did the learning investments help the enterprise to attract, develop and retain talent?*
- *Did the learning investments support the implementation of strategic business initiatives?*

Unfortunately, training expenditure is a metric still used by many human resources and training professionals, as well as some market evaluators, to measure the value that enterprises place on education and training. However, it is well known that training expenditure per person is *not* an indicator of:

- Access to training for employees.
- The quality of the training.

- The effectiveness of knowledge transfer and skill building.
- The volume of training available.
- The efficiency and effectiveness of the training function.
- The training's support of specific business goals.
- The return on investment and the impact on the business.

Therefore, I argue that training expenditure alone should no longer be used to providing a value comparison without looking at other effectiveness metrics within the education function. Between 2000 and 2007, organizations which adopted Online Learning Solutions and moved toward a more just-in-time learning environment significantly enhanced their learning capabilities. In addition, they achieved savings which translate into similar or less spending per employee, while providing their workforce with more training to support business goals, thereby, both reducing training spending levels while increasing access to learning and improving business results.

Deeper investigation might reveal which of these factors in efficiency and effectiveness support more targeted, strategic and cost-effective learning. However, at a minimum it is compelling for each individual enterprise to measure more than the simplistic data offered by overall learning investment and the number of training hours. More important is the measurement of the contribution learning is making to the achievement of strategic performance, leveraging efficiencies offered by 21st century Internet-based learning capabilities and contributing to the creation of shareholder value.

Invest on Top of the Wave

Interestingly, the same technologies that can automate and streamline a number of learning business processes, thereby reducing or eliminating inefficiencies and avoiding costs, also enable the creation of learning in the style demanded by new generations of workers, while simultaneously improving the efficiency and effectiveness of learning business processes and reducing costs.

Thanks to strong economic growth over the last couple of years, most organizations have opened up their learning budgets. However, history has shown us that waves of strong economic growth crest and ebb. Strategic leaders of learning organizations should act now to invest in capabilities that can deliver learning critical to the long-term competitiveness and survival of their companies, whether the economy – and therefore the learning budget – is up or down.

Inefficiencies in learning that are reduced or eliminated by leveraging learning technologies occur in four critical barrier areas: integration with the business, time compression to master learning, cost reduction in the delivery of learning, and quality improvements in the learning experience.

Integration with the Business

Integrating learning into practice is always a challenge. E-Learning technologies enable learning to be integrated with knowledge management and collaboration, while removing the barriers of time and location for global learners. The Internet provides the means to collect and redeploy knowledge throughout the organization.

Time Compression

The opportunity-cost limitations related to geographic location and time commitments in classroom learning are well understood. These barriers necessarily reduce the number of courses an individual can take during a year. In addition, classroom sessions often take place either too early or too late. It is too early if the skills are not practiced and immediately applied. It is too late if the learner needs to use the skills prior to attending the training program. E-Learning has significant potential to ensure that these barriers are reduced by making learning available at the time and point of need. In addition, communities of practice supported by learning technologies can allow knowledge and experience to be shared well after the end of the classroom session.

Time is more valuable today than almost any other asset. *How can e-Learning technologies ensure that the time invested brings a high return?* According to a study from the American Society for Training & Development (ASTD), the shelf life of an average training program is less than two years. Many object that version control and global deployment of courseware are time-consuming. One of the benefits of e-Learning courseware is that once a course has been updated, all employees have instant, global access to the same, most current version of a program.

Cost Reduction

The removal of barriers can potentially reduce cost, but some specific issues are directly related to cost reduction. The coordination, printing and logistics associated with the distribution of classroom training material can be time-consuming and expensive. With e-Learning, all classroom material is available online. Also, e-Learning programs usually take fewer hours to complete than a classroom event. The learners are in charge of the pace and path they use to navigate through the learning program. Also, e-Learning can be customized to a learner's specific needs. For example, conducting an online pre-assessment helps identify learning gaps so the participant can be directed to the course content needed to master a proficiency level in a particular subject area.

Quality Improvement

Finally, quality is enhanced with an e-Learning approach. Classroom materials are frequently modified by trainers for delivery in different countries and cultures. E-Learning courseware can be deployed in one version with consistent quality around the world. This is extremely important for mandated learning on regulatory requirements. E-Learning also offers potential global access to best-in-class learning content.

For most enterprises, self-service learning capabilities are still at an early stage of evolution. However, using current learning investments to target future budget fluctuations while enhancing capabilities for improved performance today demonstrates a true business savvy. It secures a competitive advantage and supports individual access to development that is less affected by downticks in the economic environment.

Interestingly, the same technologies that can automate and streamline a number of learning business processes, thereby reducing or eliminating inefficiencies and avoiding costs, also enable self-service learning. Investments in these technologies are like a magic bullet, creating learning in the style demanded by new generations of workers, while simultaneously improving the efficiency and effectiveness of learning business processes and reducing costs.

The Future of Learning and Talent Development

Live as if you would die tomorrow, learn as if you will live forever.
Gandhi

Building an Employer Brand Through Investments in Learning

A greatly underestimated area of brand image, which is critical in the recruitment and retention of premier talent, is the company brand image for career growth and development.

The brand of an organization can tell you much about its success in the market, its financial strength, position in the industry, and interesting products and services. A greatly underestimated area of brand image, which is critical in the recruitment and retention of premier talent, is the company brand image for career growth and development.

Importantly, this is in active play for those seeking an employment change and for those who are recent graduates. The best and brightest will go with a career brand that will support and develop their peak performance. . . and they know how to assess whether the brand meets their requirements. However, the challenge for those in the learning function is to ensure that the strength of their initiatives is reflected in the recruitment portfolio.

Since the global talent pool is shrinking, it demands an even more explicit communication of the strength of the *Employer Value Proposition* for new recruits, which is perceived through the *Employer Brand*. This may include:

- Inspiring culture and colleagues.
- Competitive compensation.
- International opportunities.
- Challenging career assignments.
- Investments in learning and development.
- Important career reference.

As the work environment for talent is becoming more complex and the shelf life for knowledge is accelerating – employees want to be sure that their new potential employer will help them to stay on top of the latest trends in their profession and that they will have access to knowledge for any new and upcoming career assignments. It is no surprise that recent (international) recruitment and career surveys reinforce that strong learning and development capabilities are a key differentiator for graduates to select one employer over another.

However, just investing in and enhancing unique learning capabilities alone does not necessarily guarantee that people outside the organization are aware of this aspect of the brand. According to Universum Communications (2005), *"Employer branding is a logical process through which companies reach one main goal: To have a strong appeal to their current and future ideal employees."* Learning, recruitment and HR executives must communicate strategically the important role that learning and development opportunities play in *Employer Brand* messages.

A number of things can be done in Learning and Development to support an employer-of-choice brand:

- **Develop a formal marketing and communications plan.**
  Most internal Learning functions are typically well-equipped for the development and delivery of training programs, but they lack resources with strong marketing and communication skills that can develop a plan demonstrating the value of learning for internal and external stakeholders. In contrast, 63 percent of learning functions spending over US$50 million have a formal marketing and communications plan in place.

- **Include aspects of the learning organization in company annual reports.**
  Annual reports typically include a section on Human Resources and Learning strategies and initiatives. Interestingly, 62 percent of companies formally address the learning organization/efforts in their annual report. That number rises to 79 percent for *expert* learning organizations and 88 percent for European-based companies.

- **Emphasize business leadership support of the importance of learning in their enterprise.**
  It makes a real difference if leadership at all levels in the organization embrace the importance of learning in: performance review

sessions, participation in courseware development review process, facilitating learning programs, mentioning learning in recruitment sessions, and talking about learning in new hire orientation. Currently, 54 percent of CEOs mention learning organizations in media interviews and 45 percent do so with analysts.

- **Position learning and development on the company website and in recruitment messages.**
  Leading companies have explicit messages on the company website and in recruitment collateral on learning and development, including: learning vision, overview of learning capabilities, information about their corporate university, overview of learning programs and curricula, guidelines for minimum number of learning hours annually, testimonials from participants.

- **Participate in market ranking surveys and studies**
  Survey results that generate media attention and which also have an impact on employer brand image and potential employee perception include: Top 100 Companies to Work For, Training Top 100 and Top Companies for Leaders, among others.

A company brand is one of the most import assets of an organization. Investments in people learning and development can help to enhance the employer brand and position organizations as the *Employer of Choice*. Ultimately, the CLO must position learning on the cutting-edge of 21st century capabilities while interpreting and demonstrating the value proposition to the business leaders.

Creating Value Through
Self-Service Learning

The concept of the self-service economy has been adopted widely, and as people become more and more experienced, self-service learning will be seen as just another powerful application.

The Internet has transformed the way we buy products and search for information, allowing instant access to what we need, when we need it. This self-service economy has expanded rapidly over the past few years. Now, it's learning's turn. The sole dependence on the traditional classroom has proven inefficient and ineffective, and is being replaced to some degree by self-service learning, contributing significantly to cost savings in the learning budget while improving access to high quality learning. It is estimated that Learning function overhead costs can easily range from 15 percent to 30 percent of annual learning budgets. In addition, opportunity costs are realized as learning professionals are tasked with repetitive administrative details, and employees leave their daily work to attend training.

As a result of the high delivery and opportunity costs, people generally receive approval only for the learning programs that directly support their current responsibilities. At the same time, these processes limit access to learning with two fairly serious outcomes:

- People learn skills too far in advance–or too late–to apply them effectively.
- Employees are unable to retool skill sets to accommodate rapid changes in markets, services and products.

Traditional learning business practices also limit the acquisition of new knowledge that prepares people for future assignments, ultimately impacting the business's capacity to compete aggressively in the marketplace. Moreover, today's business environment poses significant job security risks for people who do not have access to learning programs that provide opportunities to upgrade their skills.

The concept of self-service learning automates learning business processes and puts the learners in charge of their individual development. Self-service learning capabilities provide an Amazon-type look and feel, offering information about a rich variety of online learning programs and solutions. In a seamless process, learners take online assessments that result in a targeted, individual training needs analysis, automatically identifying specific courseware that meets the requirements of the individual worker. Learning programs are organized in easily accessible online curricula, which might be mapped to a competence model. People develop and maintain their learning plans online without constant interaction and support from people in the Learning function.

This self-service learning model supports several business objectives of the Learning function:

- **Operational Excellence**
  Produced by a significant reduction of administrative or transactional costs, which do not create value for the organization, combined with efficient and effective technology-supported processes.

- **Learning Excellence**
  Realized in a true strategic partnership with the business, providing learning that adds value to the business by improving bottom-line results and contributing to business transformation.

- **Performance Excellence**
  Acquired through self-service learning placed directly into the hands of the employee with just-in-time access to knowledge and skills to enhance performance or become deployable for future roles.

- **Business Excellence**
  Gained from enhanced people performance, enabling change and competitive competence in the marketplace and operational excellence, thereby creating value for the enterprise and shareholders.

The self-service learning capability is implemented by identifying and integrating learning technology platforms with e-Learning courseware, and is supported by the development of new technology-based business processes. A completely new learning culture must be established in which the learners own and are responsible for their career development, requiring significant change management efforts.

The concept of the self-service economy has been adopted widely, and as people become more and more experienced in using technology and online resources, self-service learning will be seen as just another powerful application. Much as consumers quickly learned to balance the availability and usefulness of the local bookstore with online access to books, learners will quickly demand a related self-service balance between online access to learning and the traditional classroom.

Online learning that offers instant availability of skills, knowledge and information will be blended with classroom events to enable practice of new skills, networking and sharing of information and experiences. This powerful blend will be a major driver of competitive competence for enterprises globally.

The Apple iPhone Will Shape the Future of (Mobile) Learning

No product in recent history has had more articles written before its official market launch than the iPhone. Therefore, I won't go over Its fast, menu-free, and 'dead-simple-to-operate' software, its home page with icons for the 16 functions, its spectacular and bright 3.5-inch very-high-resolution and rotating screen, nor its sleek design. More interesting is a discussion of how the iPhone (and future generations of iPhones) will shape an exciting future for learning.

In a flatter world, people need access to information, knowledge, and learning solutions at speed of business. Rapid distribution of content is critical to developing a global high performance workforce. The fast adoption of mobile phones and personal digital assistants (PDAs) has already fueled the opportunity to deliver learning on devices which are already in people's hands. Due the availability of these tools to deliver learning 'at hand', many great applications for mobile learning have been launched successfully.

However, mobile learning still experiences limitations because of technological constraints. This has changed with the arrival of the Apple iPhone. The iPhone is a multi-functional mobile device which provides tremendous opportunities to support real-time and on-the-job learning.

The most important ways the iPhone can be engaged to deliver learning and development include the capability to:

- **Utilize Google Search and Internet Access**
  On the iPhone, the Internet can be browsed and searched, knowledge management portals can be accessed, and Internet applications can be run. All of this at high speed using wireless Internet access in hot-spot areas. This transforms the experience we now have with the existing generation of PDA's where Internet applications might be slow, sometimes freeze on the device and are

hard to watch from small screens with user *unfriendly* scrolling functionality.

In addition, the iPhone provides the typical email functionality and incoming messages are fully formatted and complete with graphics, and pdf., Word® and Excel® documents can at least be opened, even if at this time not edited.

- **Broadcast Video-based Learning**
  Video recorded lectures, instructional video clips, leadership presentations, and movies can be reviewed on the iPhone. 'YouTube' style video clips can be used and viewed to provide highly engaging and motivational learning experiences.

- **Support Collaborative Learning and Social Networking**
  Learners will be able to check in with their coach, reach out to an expert or collaborate with colleagues through social networking websites and communities of practice. On the iPhone, users will be able to update a blog and contribute to a Wiki. Social networking interactions, for example through Twitter (www.Twitter.com) will be supported by a special web-based Twitter (www.twitter.com) interface that has been developed for the iPhone. This allows users to let others know *'what they are doing'*, similar to the 'Facebook' experience.

- **Create Access to Podcasts and Audiobooks**
  A growing number of employees have experienced the power of Podcasts over the past few years. Audio summaries of research studies, lectures and books provide the learner with important nuggets of learning. When there is no time to read a book – learners can listen to selections from a growing library of audiobooks on their iPhone or take foreign language lessons while commuting to work.

- **Deliver Online Learning**
  Webinars, self paced e-learning courses and virtual classrooms sessions can all be offered on the iPhone. There is only one caveat – some applications are not (**yet**) supported by the iPhone.

- **Store and View Learning Podcast Curricula**
  Learning podcast curricula can be stored on the iPhone with reference to a number of learning podcasts (audio and video based)

which are accessible from the iPhone. This will provide learners with a structured view of learning opportunities and help them to make the best podcast choices.

- **Launch and Track Assessments and Quizzes**
Learners can prepare for an exam by practicing on a variety of different tests and quizzes. Online diagnostic assessments (e.g. Emotional Intelligence, MBTI, etc.) can be completed as pre-work for blended development programs and coaching initiatives.

Although a very promising learning device, the current iPhone still lacks a number of technical features which are important for learning including: support for Flash® and Java®, video recording, memory card slot and a chat or instant message program. In addition, as we have learned from all other new learning technologies over the past decades, it will take time to experiment and explore ways to develop best practices to use the iPhone for learning.

However, I am very optimistic that additional features will be made available in future releases and that multiple iPhone-tailored web programs will be developed by different companies. The potential of the iPhone and subsequent generations of this product promise to completely transform mobile learning.

The Application of Virtual Worlds for Learning

Virtual Worlds have become increasingly popular around the world. Millions of people from all demographic backgrounds meet daily at one or more of the existing and growing 150+ Virtual Worlds. Many companies are taking virtual worlds seriously, advertising products and services, building virtual campuses, communicating with their people and setting up virtual retail stores at the pace that Starbucks is opening new coffee shops.

A virtual world (Wikipedia) is a computer-based simulated environment intended for its users to inhabit and interact via avatars (or, a graphical representation of oneself). This world is usually displayed in the form of two or three-dimensional graphical representations of humanoids (or other graphical or text-based avatars). Most virtual worlds allow for multiple users. The computer-simulated world typically appears similar to the real world, with real world rules such as gravity, topography, locomotion, real-time actions, and communication. Communication can happen through text chats or voice over IP.

Well designed virtual worlds are built on a synthesis of Web 2.0 technologies including: 3D, VOIP, chat, blogs, Wiki's, simulation applications, application sharing, advanced search capabilities, and nested IE browser that connects to the 3D world via XML.

Predecessors of today's 'virtual worlds' were computer games like Sims which moved online and emerged into Massive Multiplayer Online Games (MMOG's). The online games and simulations transferred into virtual world environments. The main purpose for virtual worlds shifted from gaming to social networking and exploration. In the virtual world people create a new life as a different person, meet and socialize with new friends from all over the world, and visit and explore new places.

A number of enterprises have been created their own virtual worlds for their (young) customers. Virtual Magic Kingdom is a virtual re-creation of Disney's theme parks. At Coca Cola's 'Coke Studios' teens can create their own customized music mixes in a virtual music studio. Also, MTV is going virtual with 'Virtual Laguna Beach'.

There is a growing interest in building internal 3D Virtual Campuses as part of a virtual world to support learning and development.

Applications for Internal Corporate Virtual Worlds include:

1. Virtual worlds to provide employees with an opportunity to meet virtually with a number of colleagues and subject matter experts, exchange information, collaborate and share new ideas. This will provide people with informal learning opportunities and support the way they learn the best . . . from other people.
2. Virtual worlds will provide a very powerful environment to get know the enterprise and the people. New orientation programs will provide online settings where you can visit different company facilities, meet with a variety of business leaders, check out the fitness room, watch videos of corporate meetings, explore achievements and experiences with different people, take a look at the latest advertising campaign, and meet new hires like yourself and launch a community.
3. Virtual worlds have become 'killer apps' for people who like to build social networks and co-create content. A number of Internet trends are merging and colliding in 3D virtual worlds. The success of MySpace, YouTube, Facebook, and Blogger has shown that there is a huge interest in building communities and sharing information. Secondly, millions of people have become co-creators of software (open source), online dictionaries (Wikipedia), and other subject areas (using wiki's and blogs). I anticipate that internal corporate virtual worlds will become part of the next generation of 'learning & knowledge management' infrastructure.
4. Internal corporate virtual worlds can include a virtual campus where employees go to take online learning, collaborate in (live) virtual classrooms, take online assessments, socialize with colleagues and share knowledge. Through the 3D user interface, more advanced training can offered through the virtual campus.
5. Virtual worlds can be used to support virtual project assignments which can be reviewed and critiqued by others in the virtual world. Such assignments could include, for example, designing a new information system, making recommendations for an enhanced business process, or offering a proposal for new communication collateral.

This will provide people with action learning experiences in a global environment.

The current online environment and potential applications of virtual worlds for learning and development are very exciting and promising. Particularly if one keeps in mind that the new generation joining the workforce has grown up with virtual worlds. It's up to CLO leadership to turn this promise into reality!

Learning at Your Fingertips

When and Where It Counts for Business Results

Fast changing competition, the introduction of new business models, legislation, globalization, and emerging technologies require employees to continually update their knowledge base and enhance their skill-set. Electronic Performance Support Systems are part of the answer and this is why the new generation of EPSSs are moving into the mainstream of learning.

Electronic Performance Support Systems (EPSS) also known as *'Process-Embedded Learning Systems'* are one of the most important capabilities in today's learning storehouse. EPSSs got their start in the past decade and provide workers access to a dynamic suite of integrated and interactive learning and support modules in the context of performing real-time work. In the simplest form, consumers use EPSSs in applications (tools) that help them to prepare a tax return, create a will, or write a newsletter.

However, the real relevance of EPSSs is in today's enterprises. People must master a vast variety of tasks which require them to follow company policies, procedures and business processes. To fulfill these tasks they are expected to master and make use of existing rich technical functionality in a broad range of software applications. This is especially true of work that requires extensive use of online templates and processes, such as ERP implementations and financial audits. However, because of the changing nature of business, organizations, and information systems, the knowledge base for job-oriented tasks and processes has a relatively short shelf-life.

In this acceleration of knowledge and process improvement, learning executives are challenged to determine which learning solution or method provides people with the information and skills needed to do their job in the most effective and efficient manner. Traditional classroom training does not adequately address the need to equip employees with the most recent knowledge in performing job-specific tasks. Typically, a skills training course is offered either *too early* or *too late* and therefore becomes less meaningful as a skill mastery solution. This is especially true, if one takes into consideration that knowledge retention from classroom training falls very rapidly. According to the Research Institute of America, only 20 percent of classroom knowledge is retained after three weeks.

On the other hand, EPSSs provide workers with a combination of information, advice and tailor-made learning interventions. Good performance support solutions offer just-in-time learning and support in a context specific (task- or job-role based) format to enable employees to do a job with minimal support, better, faster, and at less cost.

Performance support can be provided, for example, through online learning available 24/7 from the desktop, including: information, instructions, advice, data, workflows, small learning objects, diagrams, checklists, wizards, and mentors, among others. These are quickly updated with new information and technology, and can work interactively in a graphical user interface. Because these are available from the desktop, this learning operates at the center of workplace learning. EPSSs enable employees to access the most current information available and carry out job-relevant core processes and tasks without investing valuable time in a skills training class.

The key benefits of electronic performance support systems are (Desmaireais et al, 1997):

- **Increase in productivity.**
  The most important returns come from enhanced work productivity, stemming from just-in-time support and continuous learning. Additionally, EPSSs can offer a rich learning environment allowing the employee easy access to useful information that otherwise would never be consulted.

- **Decrease in costs for training.**
  The availability of an EPSS can reduce the initial training phase to the minimum set of skills required to perform the job. Workers learn the rest of the skills that are necessary for good performance by using the EPSS on-the-job.

- **Increase in autonomy of employees.**
  EPSSs provide an information rich environment in which the individual is not only better supported to perform their job but can simultaneously acquire the knowledge to improve, thus reducing the burden on support teams and allowing for greater worker autonomy.

- **Increase in quality due to uniform working processes.**
  One consequence of providing uniform information and procedures to all workers through an EPSS is a reduction of variances in workplace practices.

- **Retaining knowledge.**
  Designing an EPSS generally involves the expertise of experienced employees and formalizing the system for easy access. It also allows for the continuous addition and updates of useful information by employees. Consequently, EPSSs are a means of documenting and formalizing the knowledge capital of an organization.

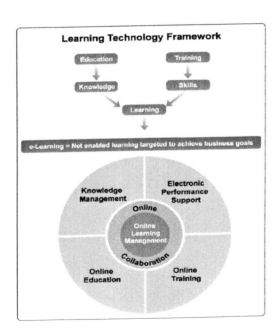

The Hudson Institute (2004) suggests that only 20 percent of today's workforce has the skills for 60 percent of the jobs in the year 2020. Fast changing competition, the introduction of new business models, legislation, globalization, and emerging technologies require employees to continually update their knowledge base and enhance their skill-set. Electronic Performance Support Systems are part of the answer and this is why the new generation of EPSSs are moving into the mainstream of learning. Over the recent years, a number of vendors have specialized in the development of company specific and cost effective EPSSs, which support learning where it counts: in the workplace and just-in-time!

Interestingly, online performance support solutions can be blended with other learning solutions, such as: self-paced e-learning courses, recorded virtual classes, live webinars, workshops, or even classroom courses to provide a high level introduction. EPSSs are included in the portfolio of online learning solutions shown in the Learning Technology Framework, including: online training, online education, knowledge management, online collaboration and online learning management.

The DNA of the Talent Enterprise in 2020

Key elements of the DNA of the Talent Enterprise will be entrepreneurship and accountability at all levels. Knowledge will flow freely throughout the enterprise and there will be a strong informal coaching and mentoring culture in place.

The employee scenario is experiencing vast changes that will transform the enterprise landscape in the next decades. By 2020 most of the baby boomers, born between 1946–1964 and the largest generation in the workforce, will enjoy retirement. Many countries, including China which will by then be the largest economy in the world, will be experiencing a steady decline in their workforce. Generation Internet (born after 1980) will play a dominant role in enterprises. The impacts on organizational culture, strategies and learning will be enormous, and enterprise-wide strategies will be driven by the ability to attract and retain talent and the challenges in this arena are mounting.

Already this is beginning. Multiple Llayers of management have experienced a significant decline because of the desire to obtain *'flatter'* organizational structures in the effort to become more agile and the Internet has automated many typical management tasks. This is further impacted by the current generations of talent who want to operate more autonomously and don't need or desire to be 'managed'.

As this trend continues into the future, the role of management and the related organizational structures will change even more. In the new talent enterprise of 2020, knowledge workers will define their own roles, activities and set their own compensation. Compensation will be a function of measurable contribution to the results of the enterprise using metrics which everybody has agreed to and that support desirable profitability levels. This will enable talent to work the number of hours they want to and will provide people with maximum flexibility. Successful enterprises will be successful in developing a culture that has attracted and retained women at all levels. Leading value-based enterprises do not just make a contribution to shareholders but also benefit the welfare of overall society. Employees will have a number of opportunities to contribute to activities which are supplemental to the overall business.

People will focus their development not any longer on weaknesses but focus on the development of their strengths. Top performers will only be promoted into roles where they can continue to leverage their strengths. Traditional career and promotion paths will have been replaced by development opportunities which support each individual's unique strengths and their inherent talents. Other elements of the DNA of the Talent Enterprise will be entrepreneurship and accountability at all levels. Knowledge will flow freely throughout the enterprise and there will be a strong informal coaching and mentoring culture in place. Design and innovation will be significant drivers of the enterprise core competencies.

How Will We Learn in 2020?

Learning will change and become more self-directed and technology – focused. The next generation of search engines will provide people with results for all internal and external sources and search words will have been automatically tagged. New learning intelligence applications will push Information and learning objects to people based on personal knowledge profiles which will be updated automatically.

Leading enterprises will launch 3-D virtual organizations comparable to *Second Life* (www.secondlife.com). Second Life is a 3-D virtual world entirely built and owned by its residents. Since opening to the public in 2003, it has grown explosively and is inhabited by millions of people from around the globe.

Enterprise-wide tailored 3D virtual environments will replace content, knowledge management and learning systems. Potential hires will learn about available positions, experience different jobs, collaborate with colleagues and learn anywhere in the organization. Business leaders will engage globally in virtual teams and simulate online business options. Employees will team up globally on many projects and create and share knowledge.

Learning and work will be integrated to a great extent. E-Learning 4.0 has arrived and learning at employee's fingertips will have become a reality. The next generation of iPhones will be one of the leading devices for learning. Informal learning accessed anywhere, anytime will have eclipsed formal learning in frequency, time allocated and focus, and the more formal learning events will intentionally focus on face-to-face knowledge sharing and networking.

The described online learning and collaboration environment will provide the maximum in 'High Tech' development opportunities. However, in this Internet Age there will be a growing need for groups to engage in 'High Touch' time spent working and learning face-to-face. In dynamic classroom environments, groups will step away from the virtual world and their digital devices to dedicate time to reflect, to leverage individual and collective talents to the maximum, and to build sustainable relationships and networks. In conclusion, the ultimate learning vision is a well balanced and blended *High-Tech - High Touch* approach with a strong emphasis on exploring individual personal growth and development.

Where Are We Today?

Thanks to the Internet, a myriad of learning solutions have emerged over recent years, supporting both formal and workplace learning.

Formal Learning Programs relate to specific learning objectives and typically include instructional design approaches, while workplace learning or *self-directed learning* supports informal learning and must be crafted to purpose, but does not require specific instructional learning design.

Spectrum of Formal and Workplace Learning

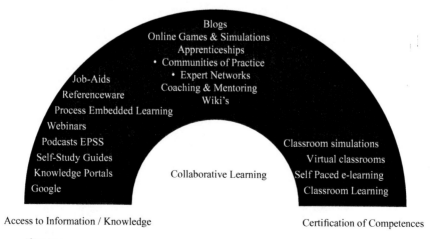

A number of integrated learning solutions provide people with access to information/knowledge. Whereas people in the past searched in books and with colleagues and friends for knowledge, today Google has become the *killer application* for learning. Podcasting, both for sound and video, has been launched by many enterprises and proven to be a very effective medium to for sharing knowledge with a younger generation, as universities are leveraging the ubiquitous iPod® and its competitors to provide students with access to curricula and online lectures.

Collaborative learning applications, including communities of practice, expert networks, and online simulation, are experiencing rapid growth and will have a strong future as they support the team-based learning style of Generation Internet. The classroom has been transformed in many organizations from lecture-based and PowerPoint® driven events toward a facilitated learning continuum. Classroom simulations and expert performance coaching provide people with a real work experience in a safe environment.

Most enterprises are in the process of defining a new learning strategy that will provide knowledge and skills to their people when they need it. All learning solutions shown in the visual above will be part of the extended 'blend' of learning. In evaluating the best learning solutions, a number of criteria will be taken in consideration, including but not limited to:

- Business impact of the learning
- Learning effectiveness
- Costs for development and deployment
- Main objectives of specific learning interventions
- Best medium for the best content
- Learning styles of people
- Shelf-life of learning solutions
- The need for global and 24/7 access
- Certification and compliance requirements
- Technology environment/Internet access and bandwidth
- Impact on company culture

A very interesting journey in place for enterprises are able to do this well and these will be the winners in the knowledge economy – able to attract and develop and retain top talent.

A striking affirmation of the value of learning comes in a statement from the former Secretary-General of the United Nations, Kofi Annan.

"Education is an essential human right, a force for social change – and the single most vital element in combating poverty, empowering women, safeguarding children from exploitative and hazardous labour and sexual exploitation, promoting human rights and democracy, protecting the environment and controlling population growth. Education is a path toward international peace and security."

It is the future of universally accessible and empowering learning that is the focus of my work and life, and is the reason why this book and all of the royalties it may generate are dedicated to our children and their parents around the world.

e-Learning for Kids Foundation

You must give some time to your fellow men. Even if it's a little thing, do something for others – something for which you get no pay but the privilege of doing it.

Albert Schweitzer

All royalties from this book will be donated to the **e-Learning for Kids Foundation (www.e-learningforkids.org)** a non-profit, global foundation that provides free, high quality online learning to all children around the world.

e-Learning for Kids is dedicated to fun and free learning on the Internet for children ages 5–12. Established in late 2004, our vision is to be *the* source for childhood learning on the Internet – available from anywhere and without charge. The Foundation offers best-in-class, free courseware in math, science, reading, health and computers; and a community for parents and educators to share innovations and insights in childhood education.

Currently, more than 35 e-Learning-related companies, associations and NGOs, and over 70 individuals are sponsors and supporters of the Foundation. In addition, an all-volunteer staff of education and e-Learning experts and business professionals from around the world work tirelessly to make a difference for children with access to learning.

Help Us to Open More Doors for Kids

e-Learning for Kids is actively seeking collaboration with innovative companies, e-Learning vendors and experts to accelerate our vision, to share courseware and content, to reach out through e-Learning and children's media, and to provide access to online learning through technology and infrastructure.

- **Visit Our Website and Learn With Your Children.**

- **Tell Others about e-Learning for Kids**
  - Parents, Teachers and Schools
  - Other Organizations Who Work with Children
  - Link an e-Learning For Kids Banner to a Website or Blog

- **Join Our Team of Volunteers**
  - Become a Country Representative
  - Translate a course (4–8 Hours): Spanish, French, Mandarin
  - Participate in Quality Review Teams: Kids and Adults

- **Offer Your Support**: See Our Website to Make a Tax Deductible Contribution

- **Become a Sponsor**

For more information, please visit www.e-learningforkids.org or send an email to: info@e-learningforkids.org

Proud Sponsors and Partners of the e-Learning For Kids Foundation (as of March 2008)

Sponsors and Partners

- Allen Interactions
- Aptara
- Articulate
- Convergys
- Deloitte
- Enspire Learning
- Executive Learning Exchange
- FCS
- GlobalEnglish
- GoodSearch
- Graphik Connexions
- IBM
- icedr
- InterimIC
- Intrepid Learning Solutions
- Harvard Business School Publishing
- Kupa
- KnowledgeAdvisors
- LatitudeU
- LearningGuide Solutions
- Learning.Net
- Liquid Animation
- MicroPower
- ProtonMedia
- Quest Software
- QuickMind/QuickLessons
- Quistor
- Rotary Club of Winnetka/Northfield
- Saba
- SkillSoft

- Stoas
- Symbiosis Centre For Distance Learning
- The eLearning Guild
- Elliott Masie's Learning CONSORTIUM

Media & Outreach Partners

- American Society of Training and Development
- CHECKpoint eLearning
- CLO Magazine
- Full Circle Communications
- ICWE GmbH
- Intellectueel Kapitaal
- Learning Review
- WebEducativa.net

NGO Partnerships

- Close The Gap (www.close-the-gap.org)
- LINGOS (www.lingos.org)
- Save The Children (www.savethechildren.org)
- SchoolNetAfrica (www.schoolnetafrica.net)
- CII-Shiksha India Trust (www.shikshaindia.org)
- To Be Worldwide (www.tobeworldwide.org)
- Viafrica (http://www.viafrica.org/)
- One Laptop per Child (http://laptop.org/)

About the Author

Nick van Dam is an idea generator, visionary, consultant and thought leader.

Nick is the Global Chief Learning Officer for Deloitte and advisor for the Deloitte Consulting Human Capital Practice. As an internationally recognized consultant and thought leader in Learning and Talent Development, Dr. van Dam has written articles and has been quoted by The Financial Times, Fortune Magazine, Business Week, Management Consulting, Learning & Training Innovations Magazine, T+D Magazine, Bizz Magazine, and The India Times, among others. He is a columnist for CLO Magazine (US) and Intellectueel Kapitaal Magazine (The Netherlands). He has authored and co-authored a number of books including:*Organisation & Management, an international approach*, 1991–2007 (Dutch and English), *Business Simulations-Topsim Series*, 1995, *Change Compass*, 2001, *The e-Learning Fieldbook*, 2004 and 2006 (Mandarin Edition), and *The Business Impact of e-Learning*, 2005.

He holds several advisory board positions including among others, The International Consortium for Executive Development and Research (ICEDR), Lexington, MA/USA, a global learning alliance of some 40 of the world's leading companies and 25 premier business schools.

He is founder and chairman of e-Learning for Kids Foundation, which is a global non-profit foundation (www.e-learningforkids.org) that provides schools and children around the world with free Internet-based courseware.

Dr. van Dam is a graduate of the *Vrije Universiteit van Amsterdam*, Bachelor Degree in Economics and Pedagogy, and holds a Master Degree in Organization and Management from the *Universiteit van Amsterdam*. He earned his doctorate in Business Administration at *Nyenrode Business University, Breukelen*, The Netherlands.

For more practices on Learning & Talent Development visit: www.nickvandam.com.

Notes & Take-Homes